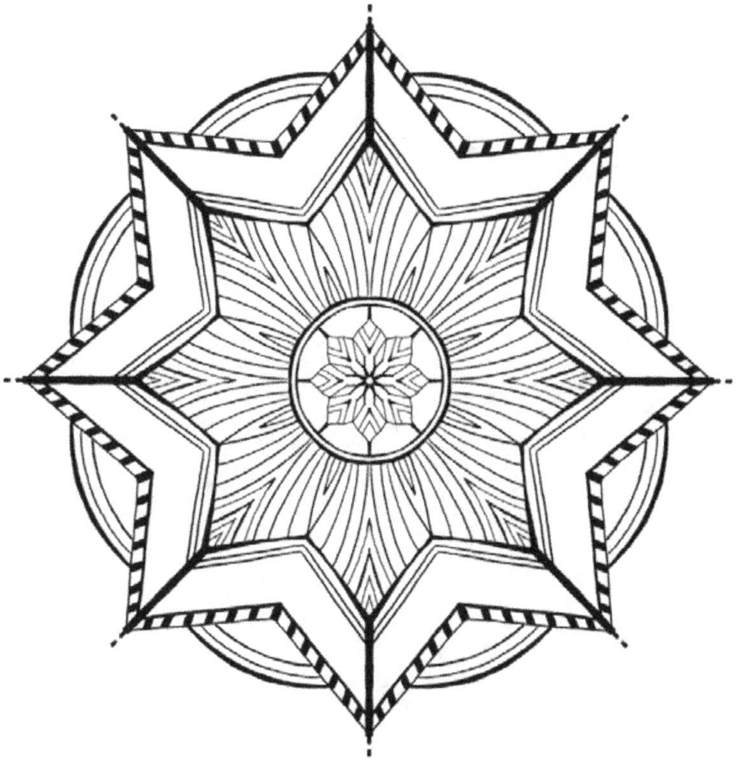

Mandala

coloring book for Kids

This book belongs to

____

____

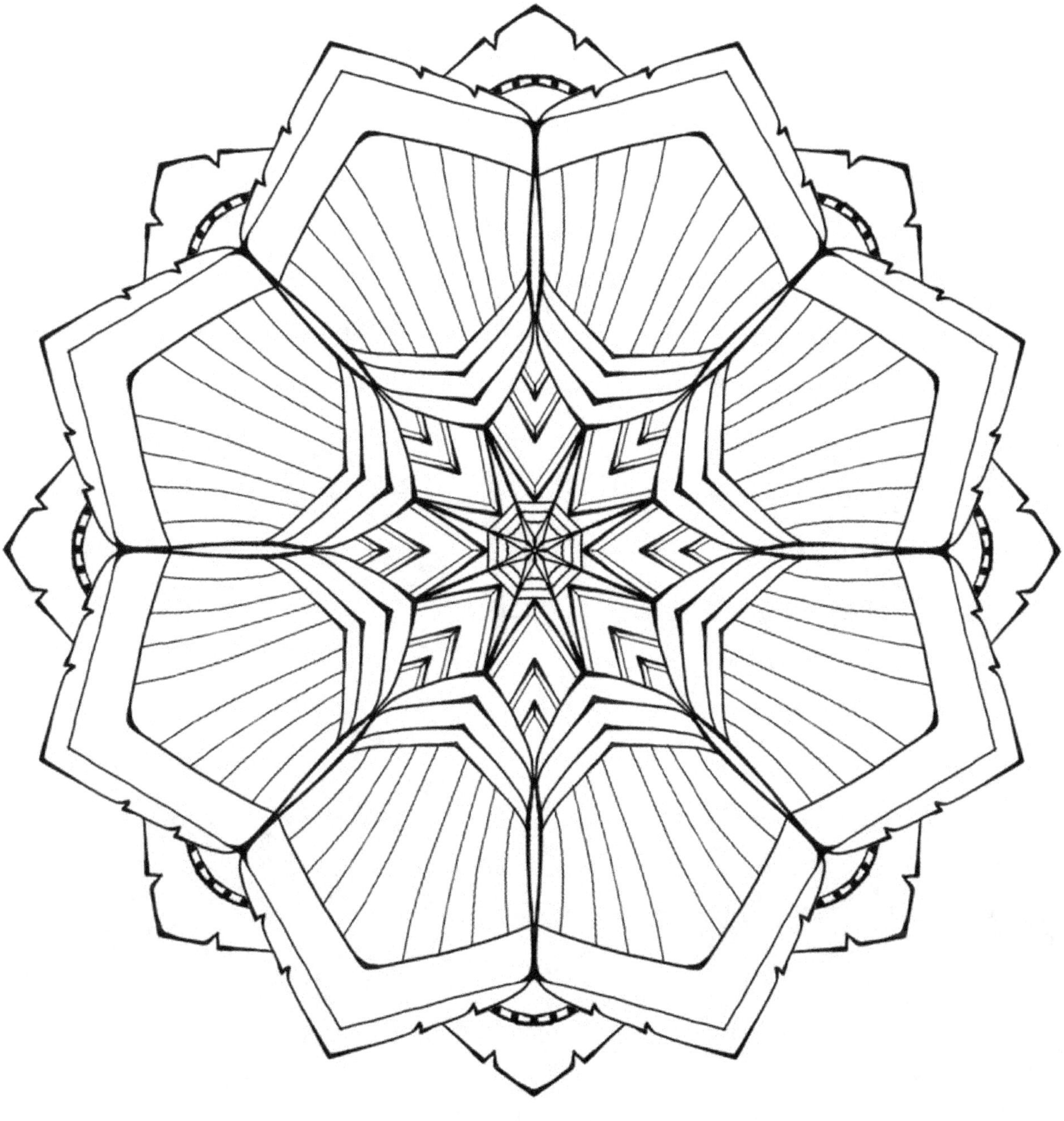

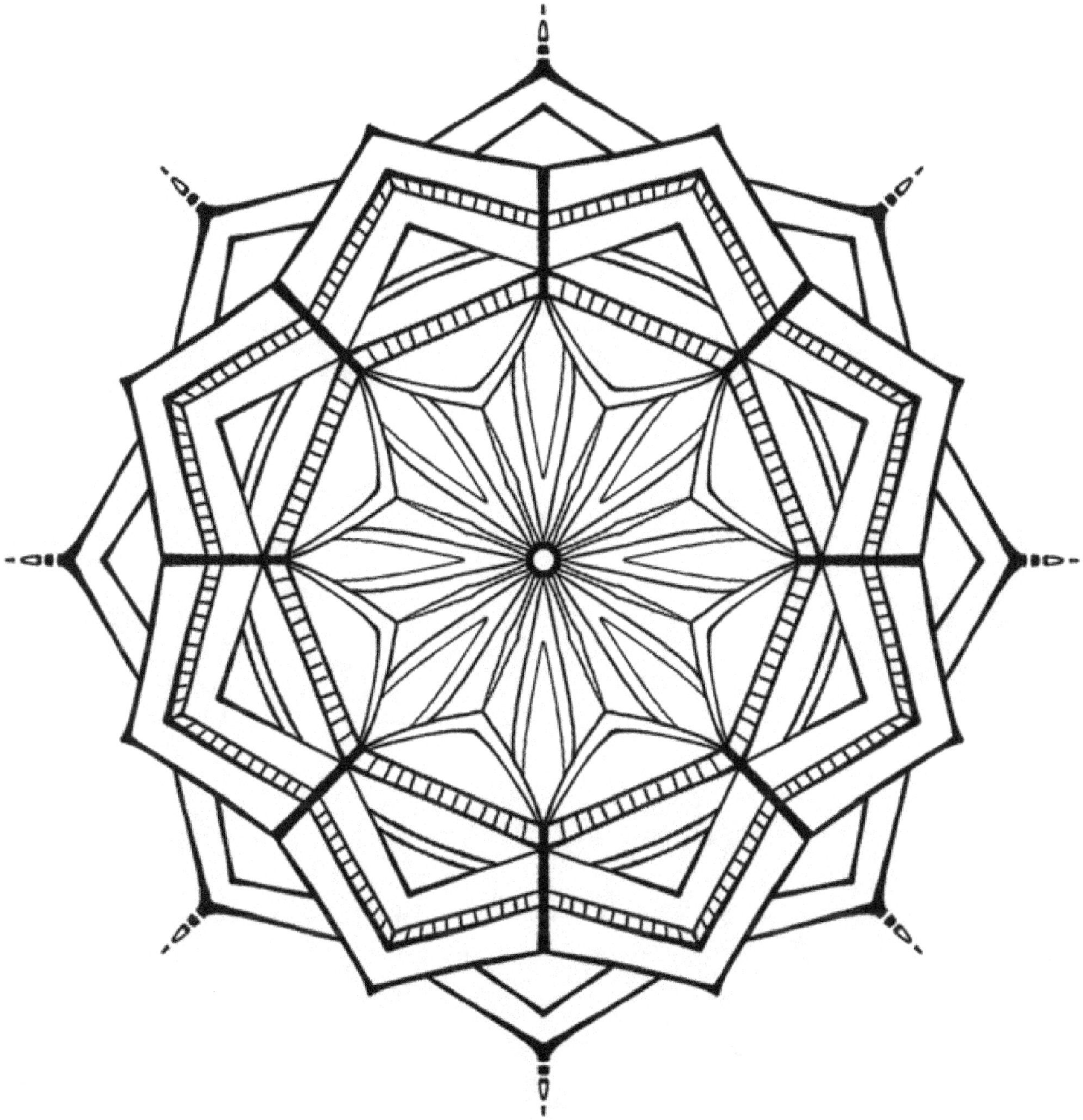

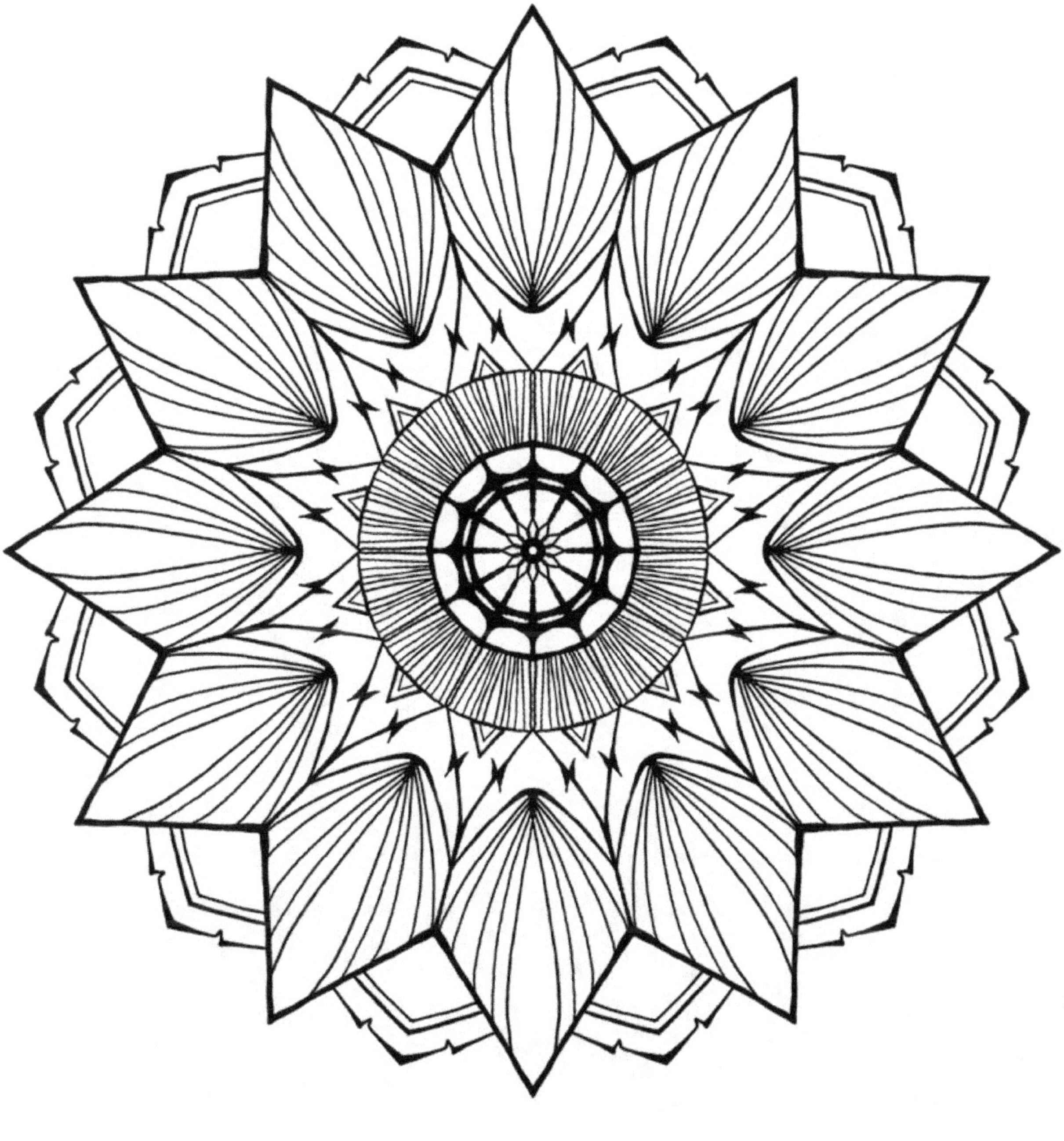

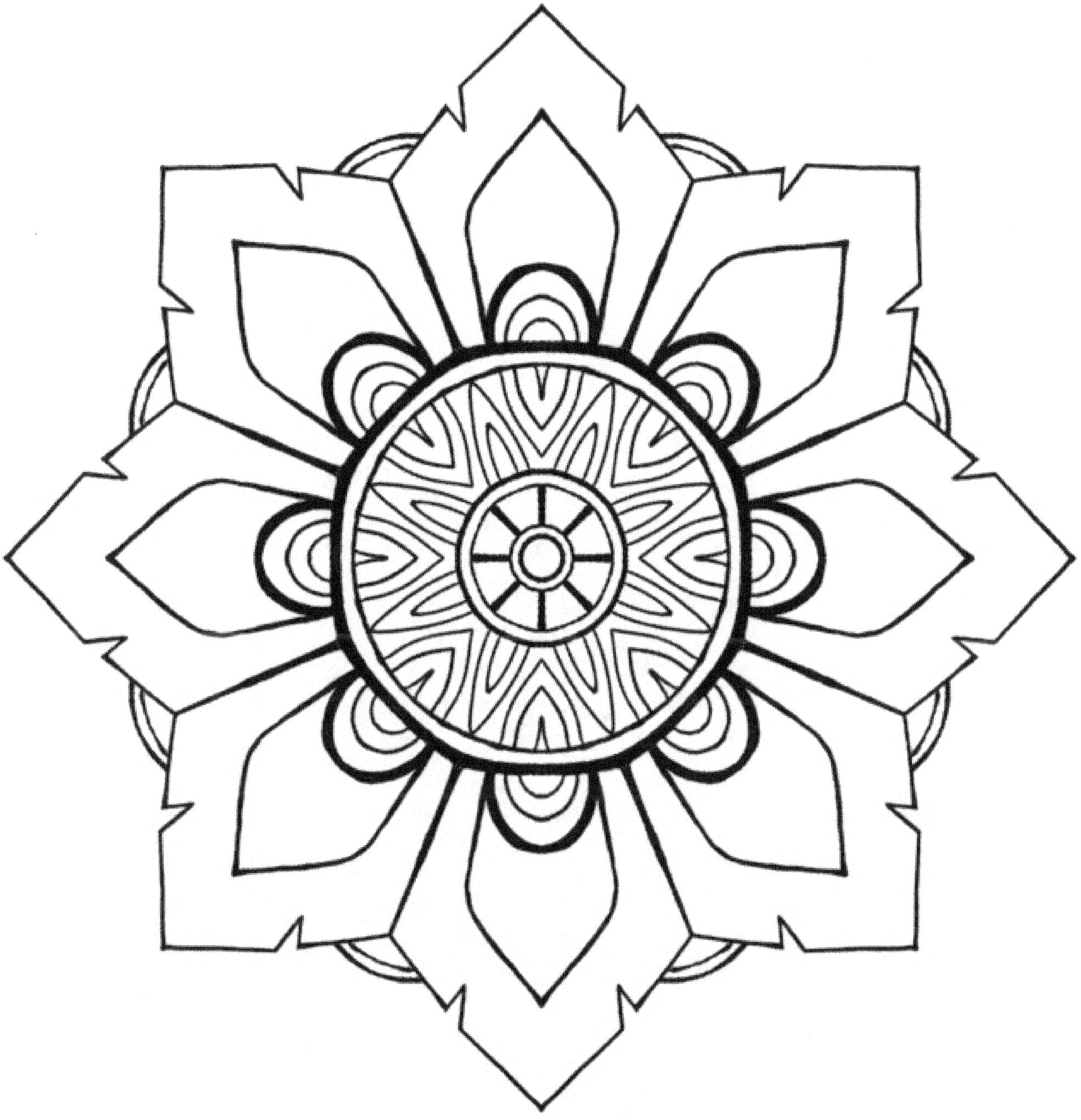

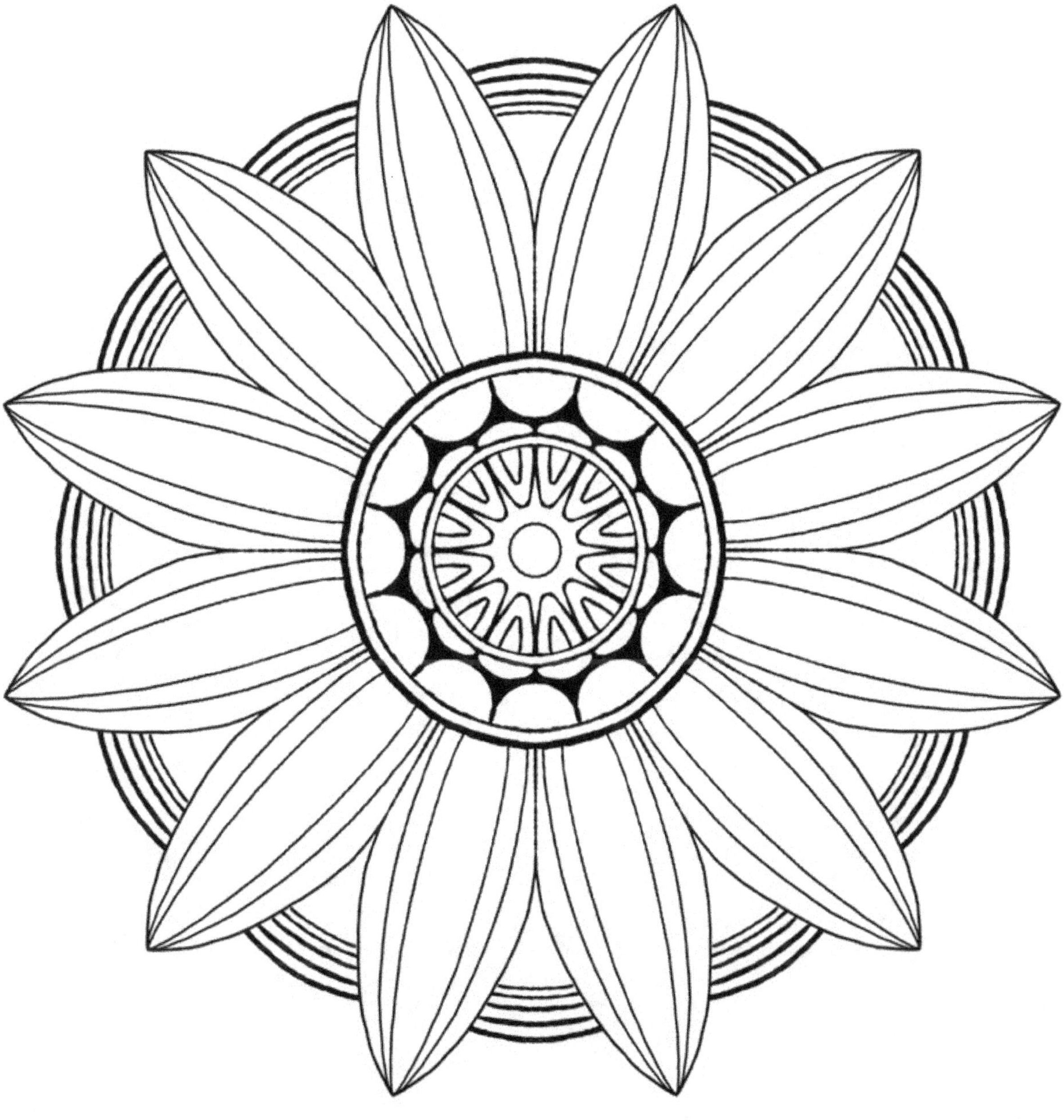

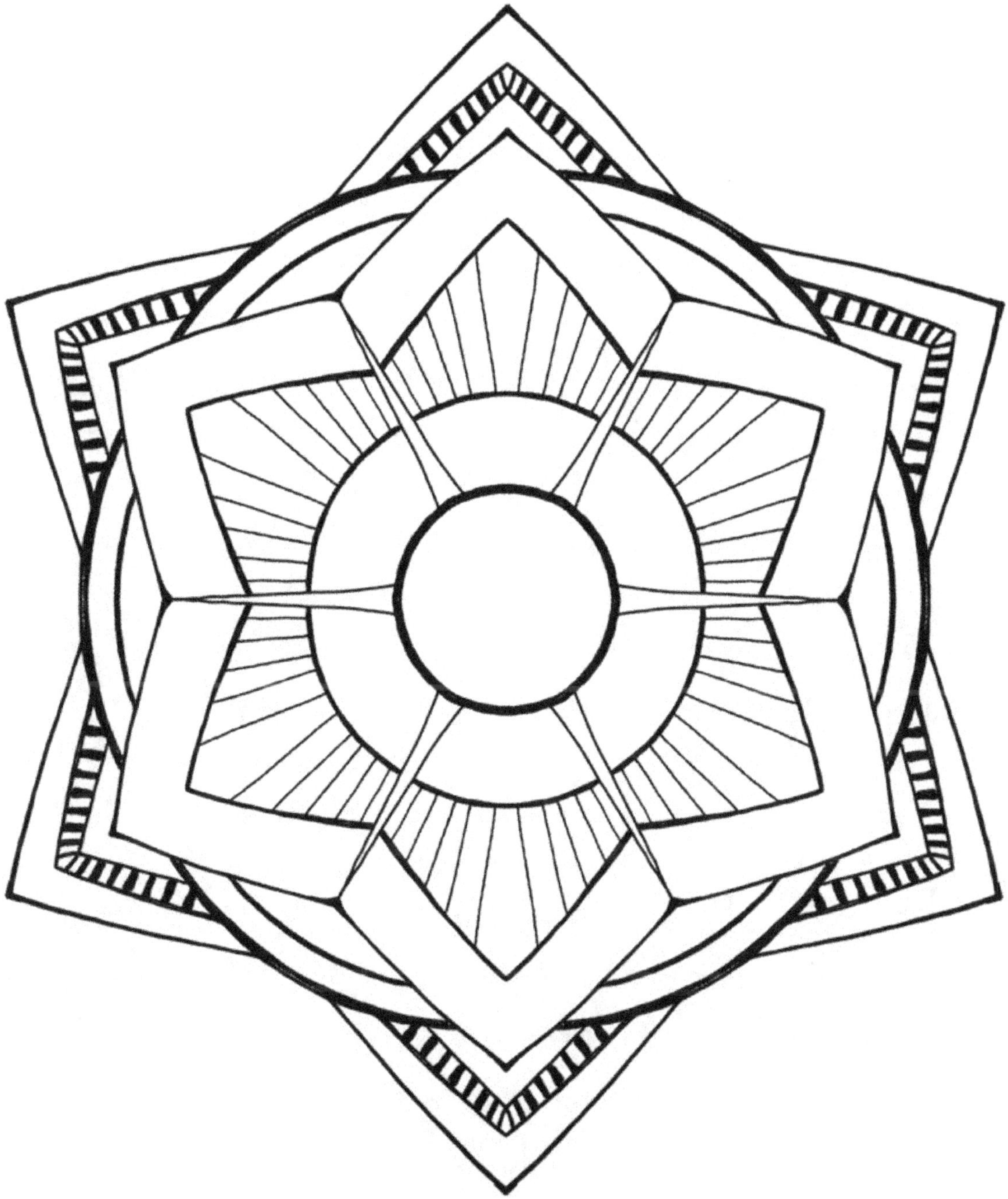

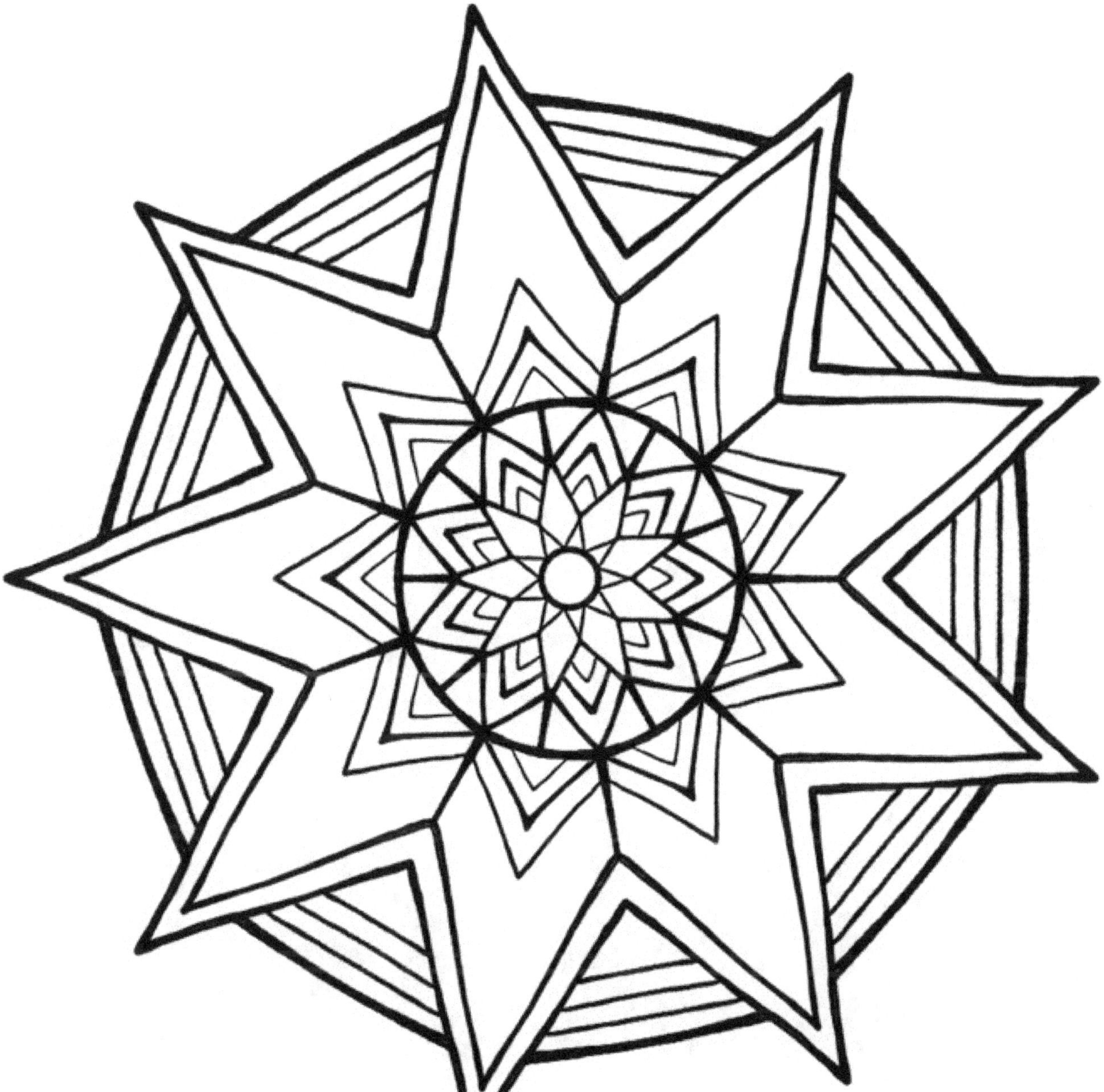

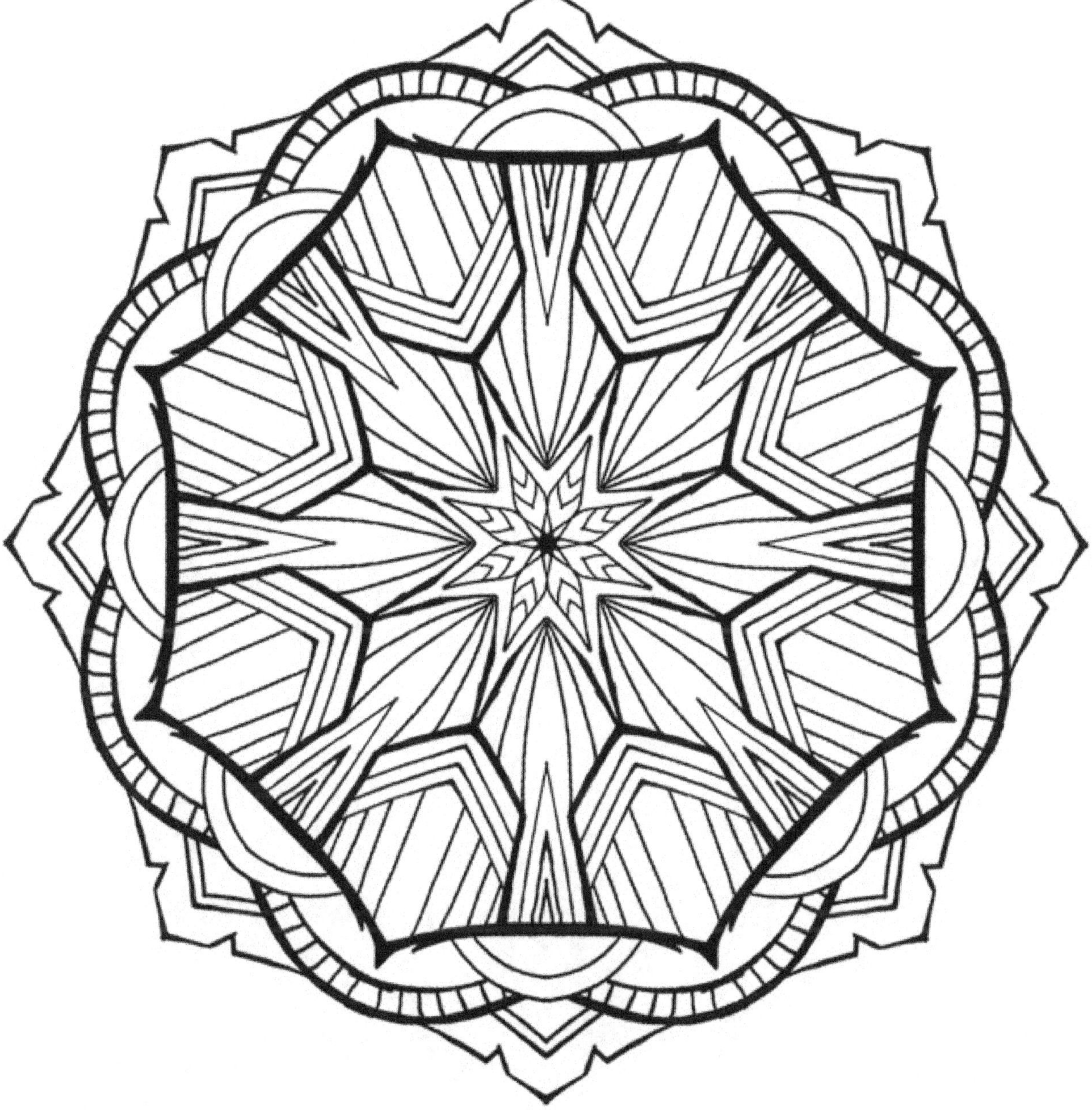

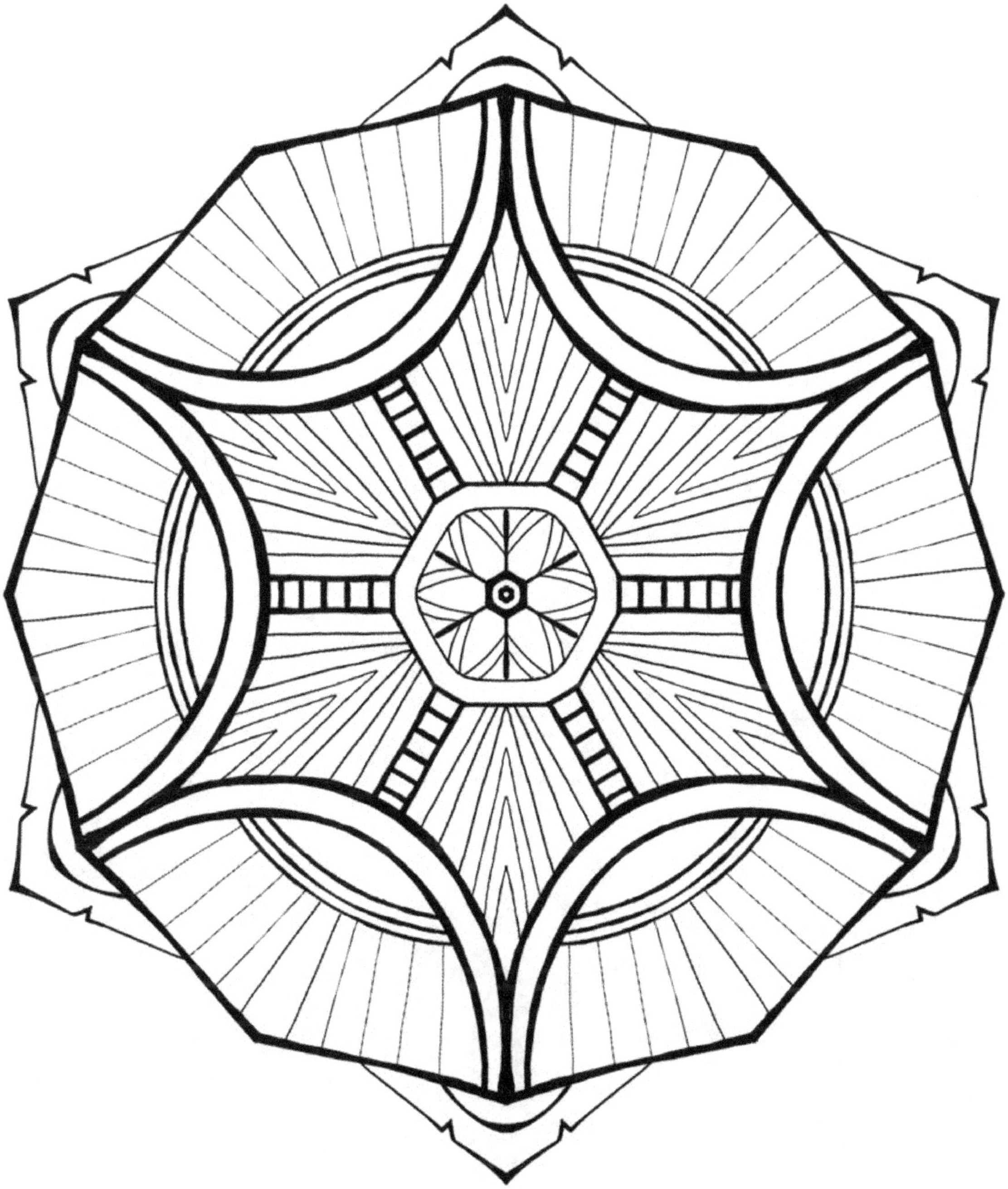

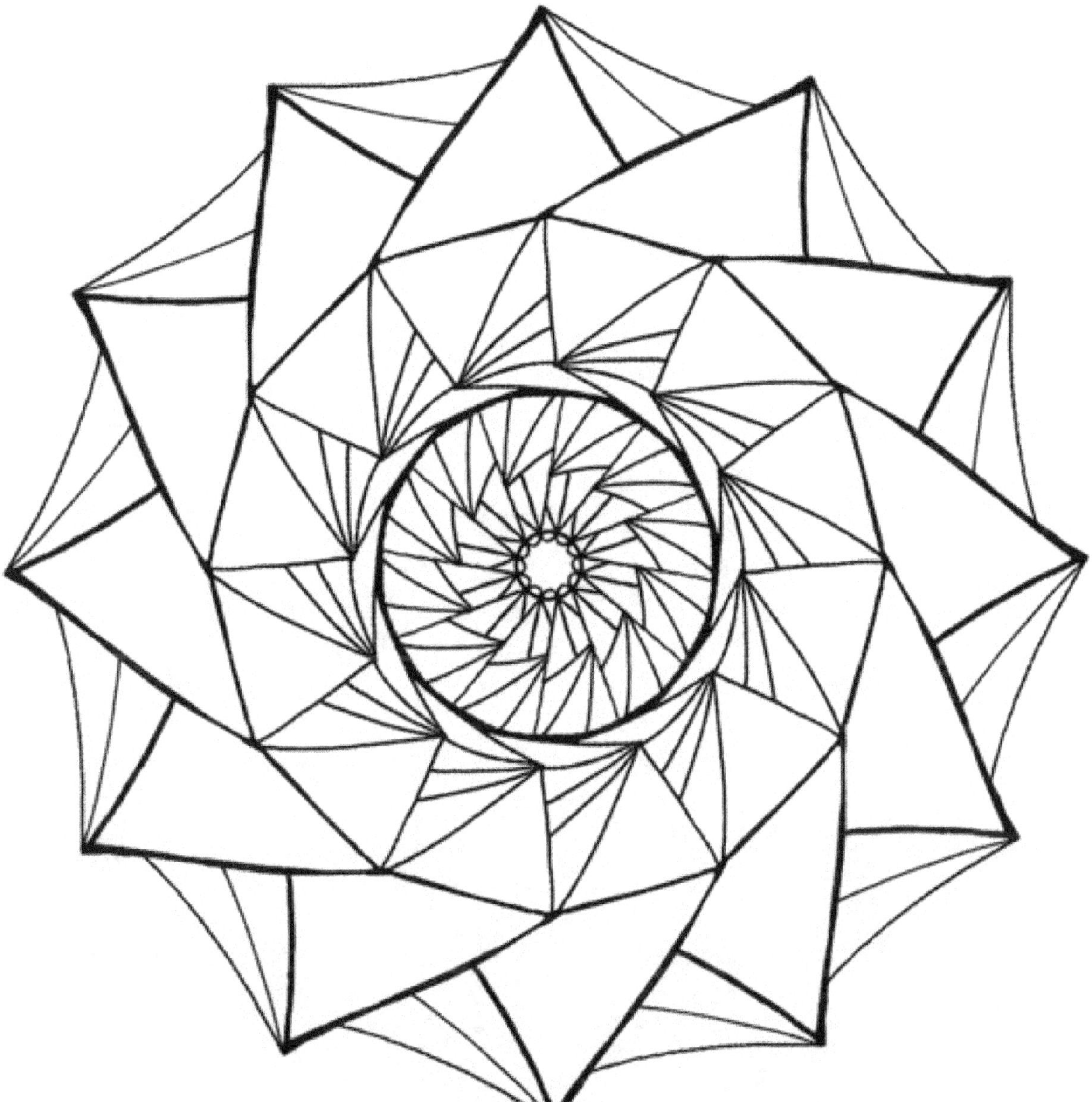

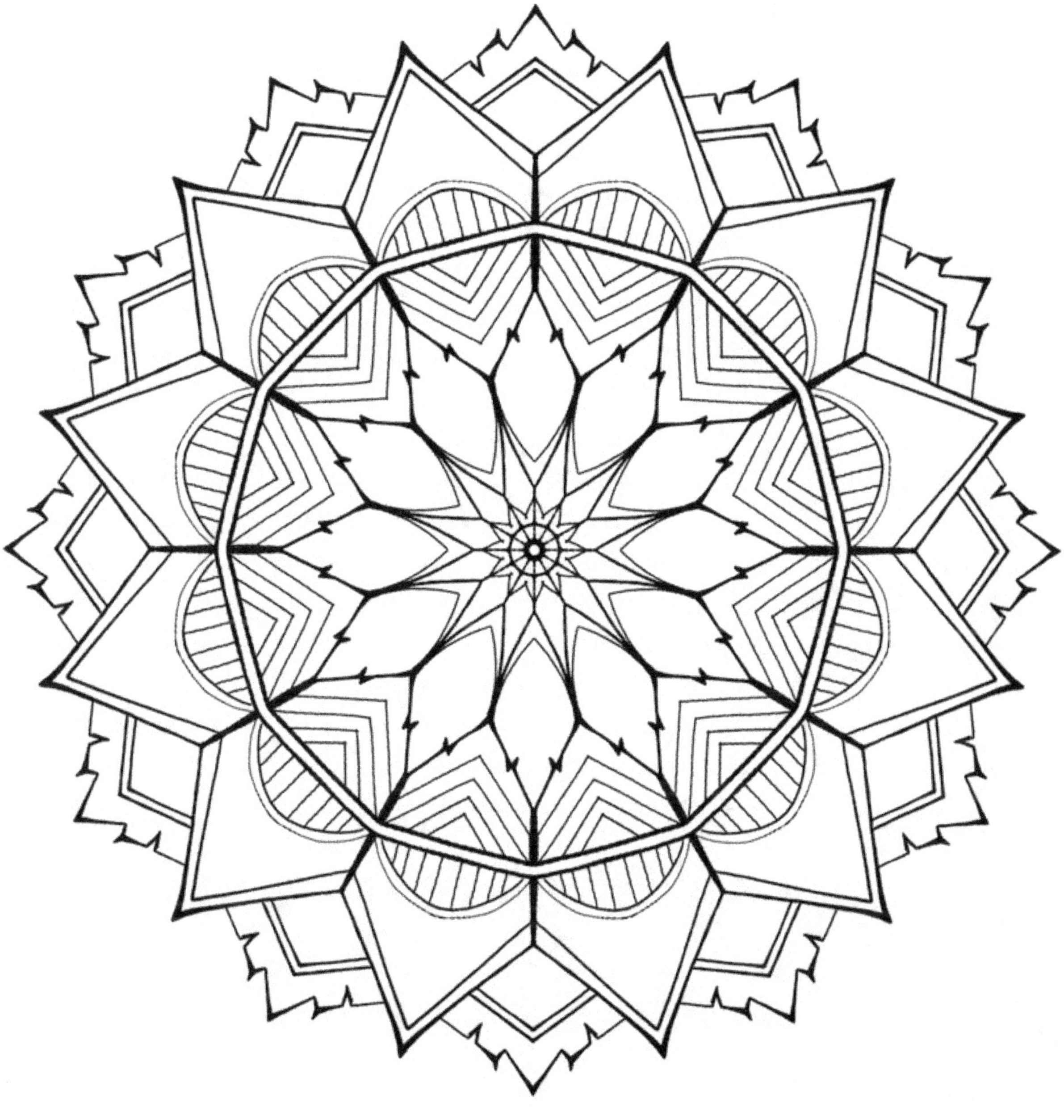

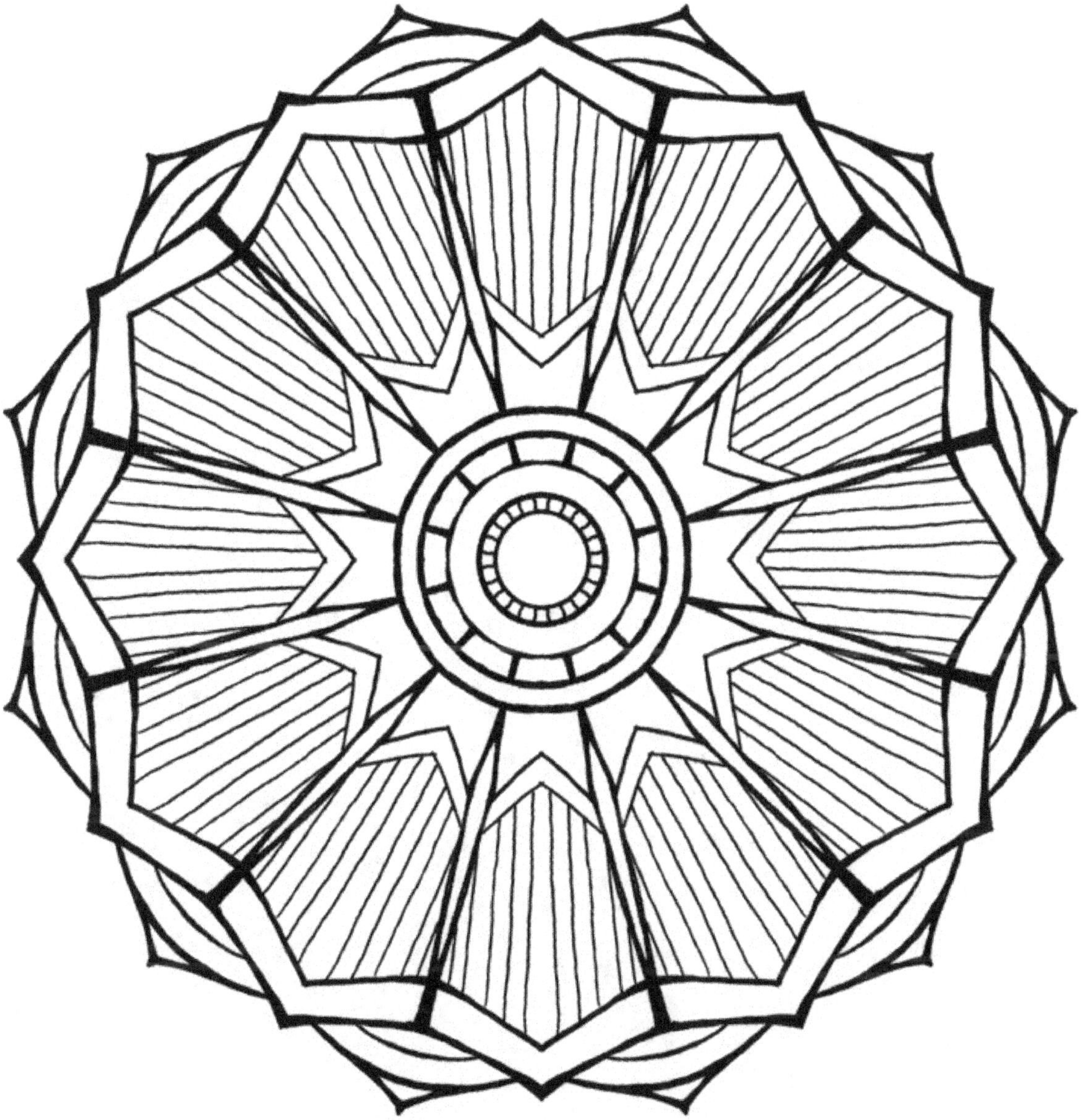

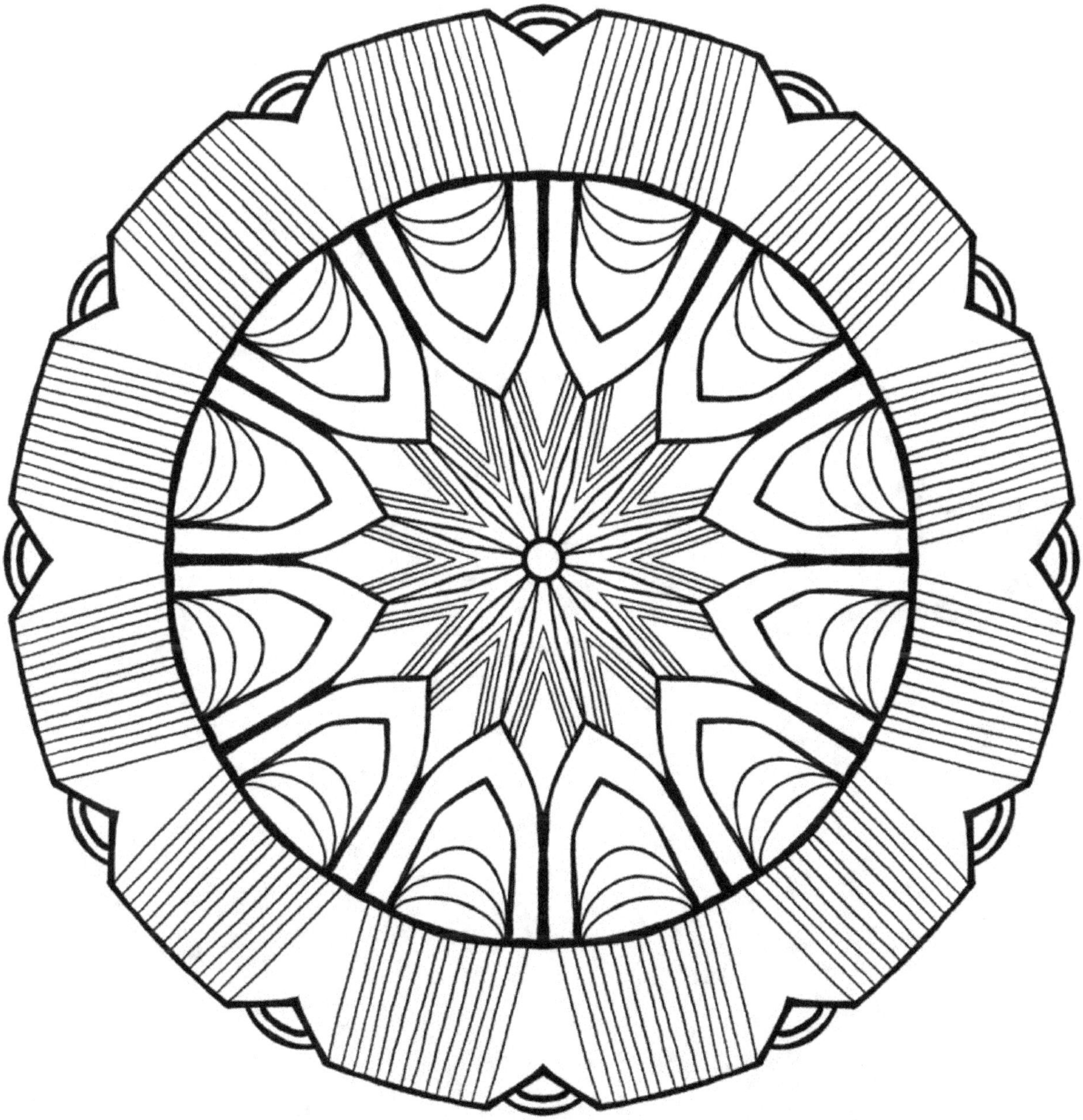

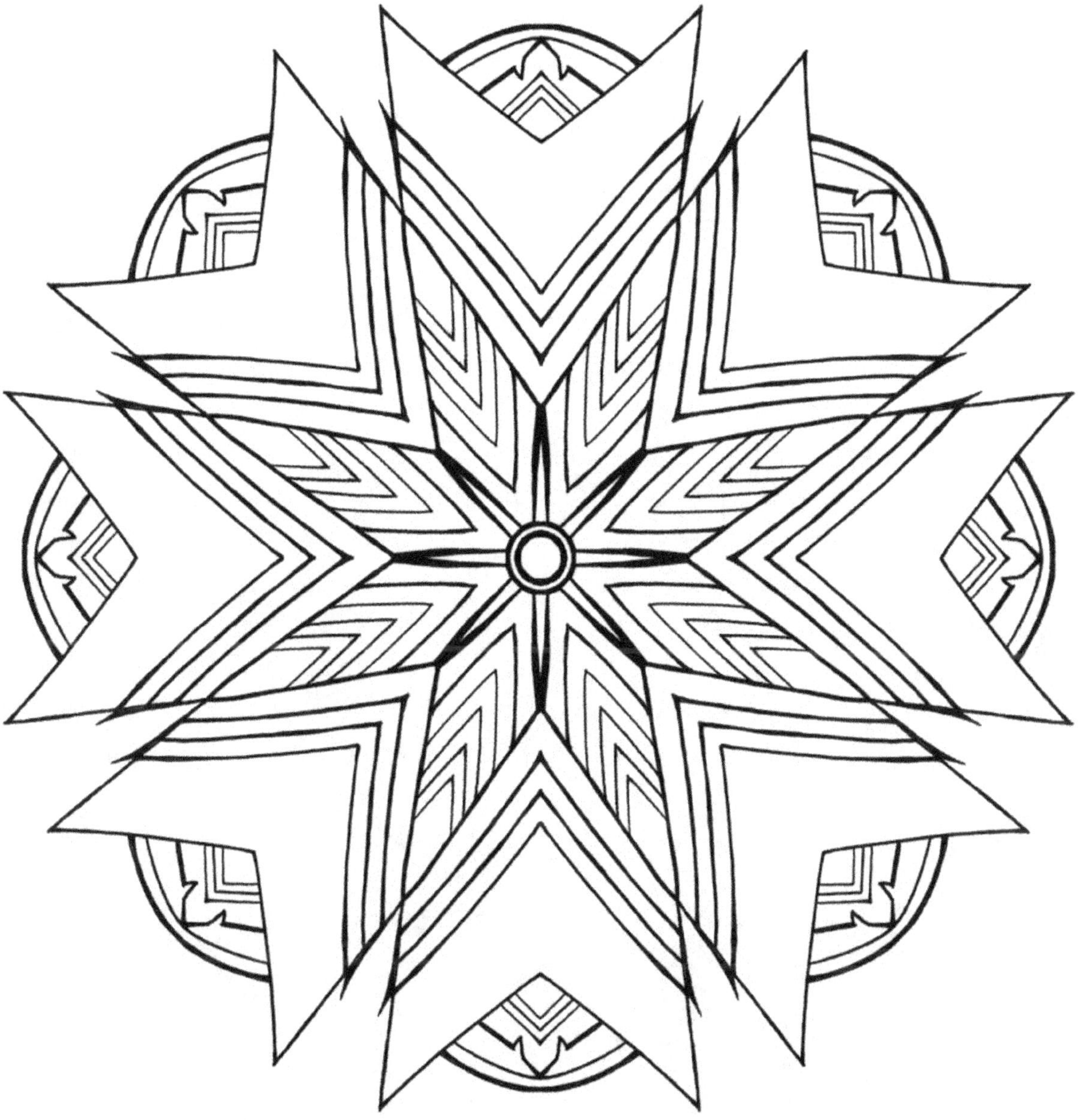

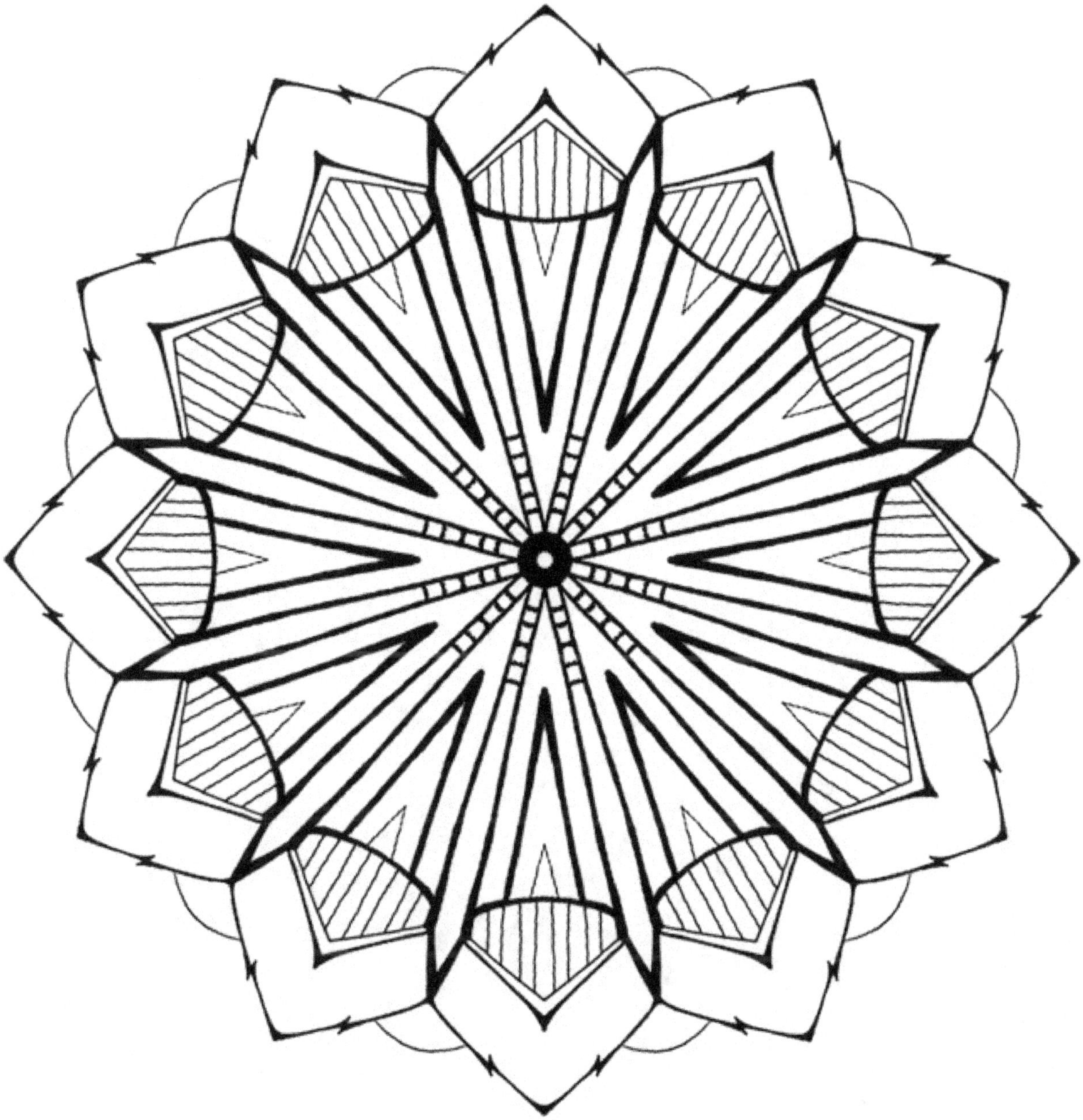

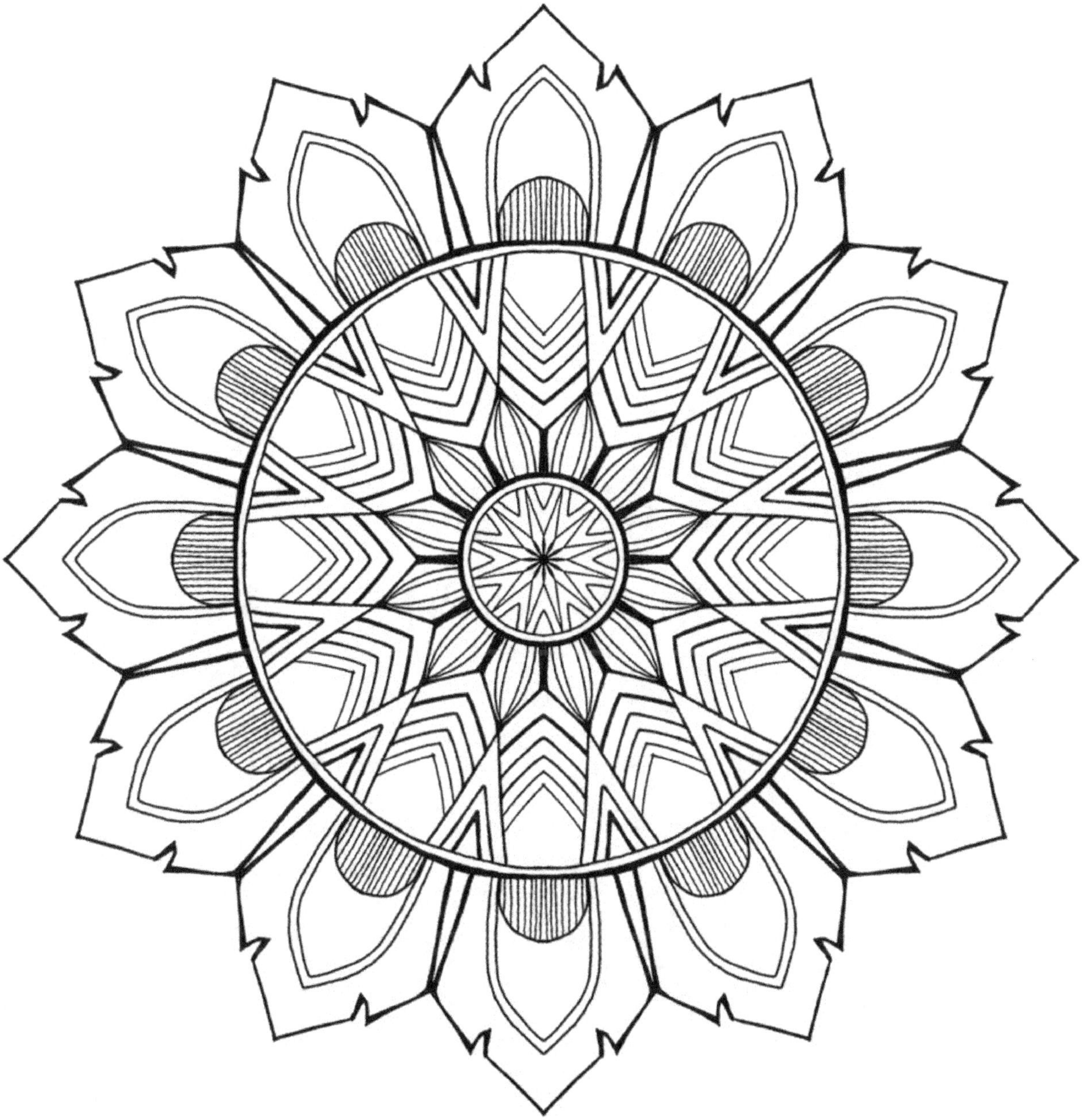

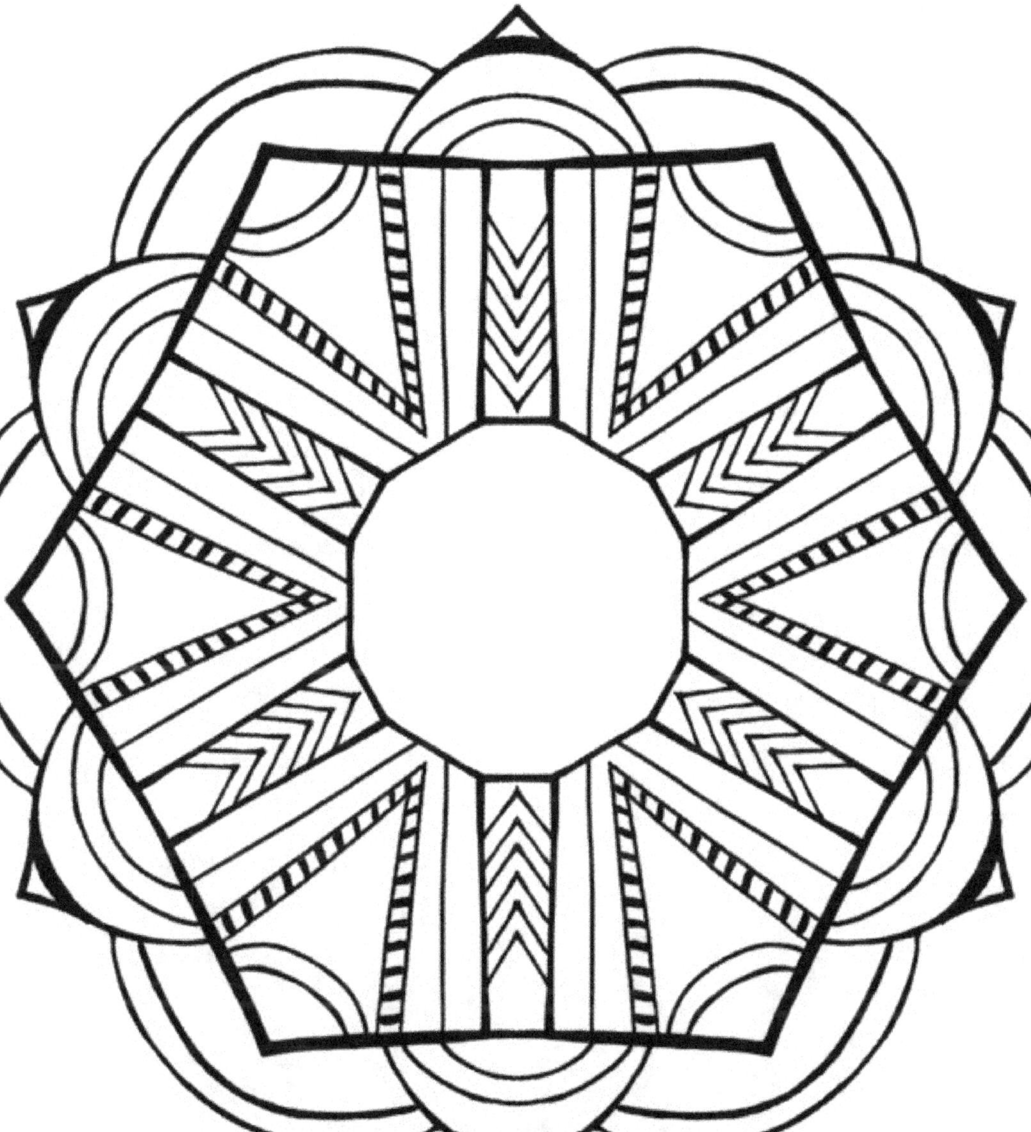

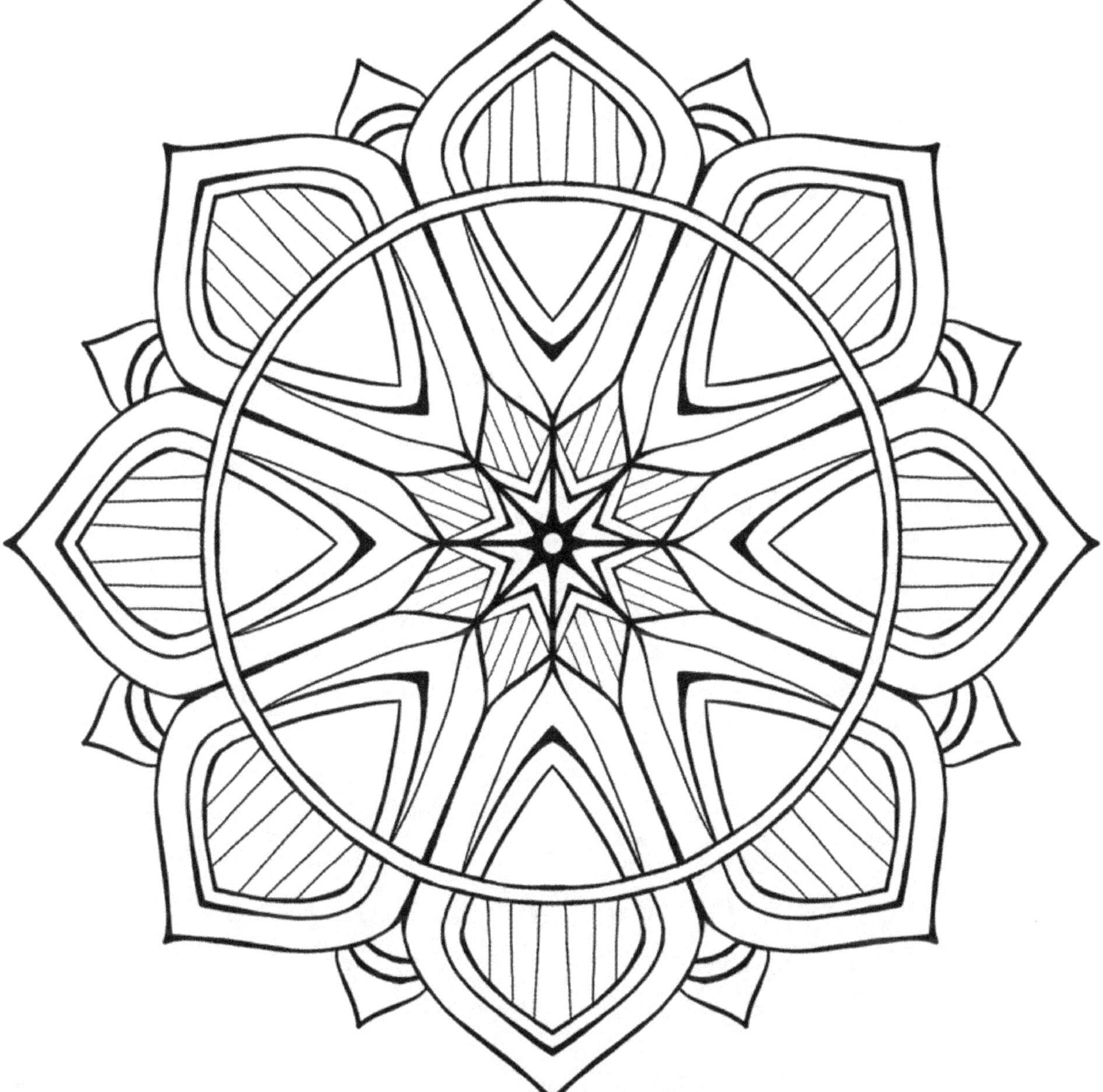

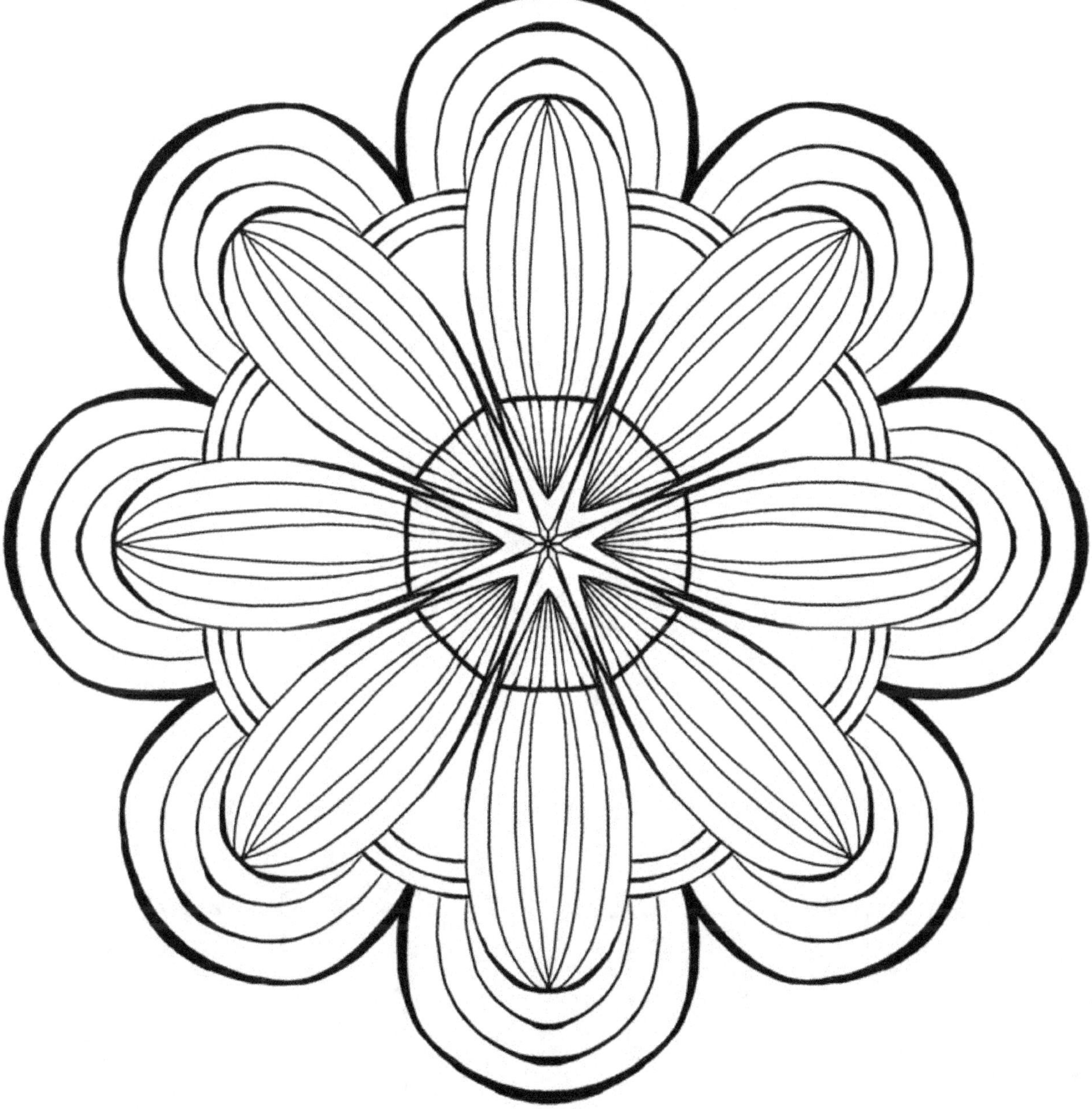

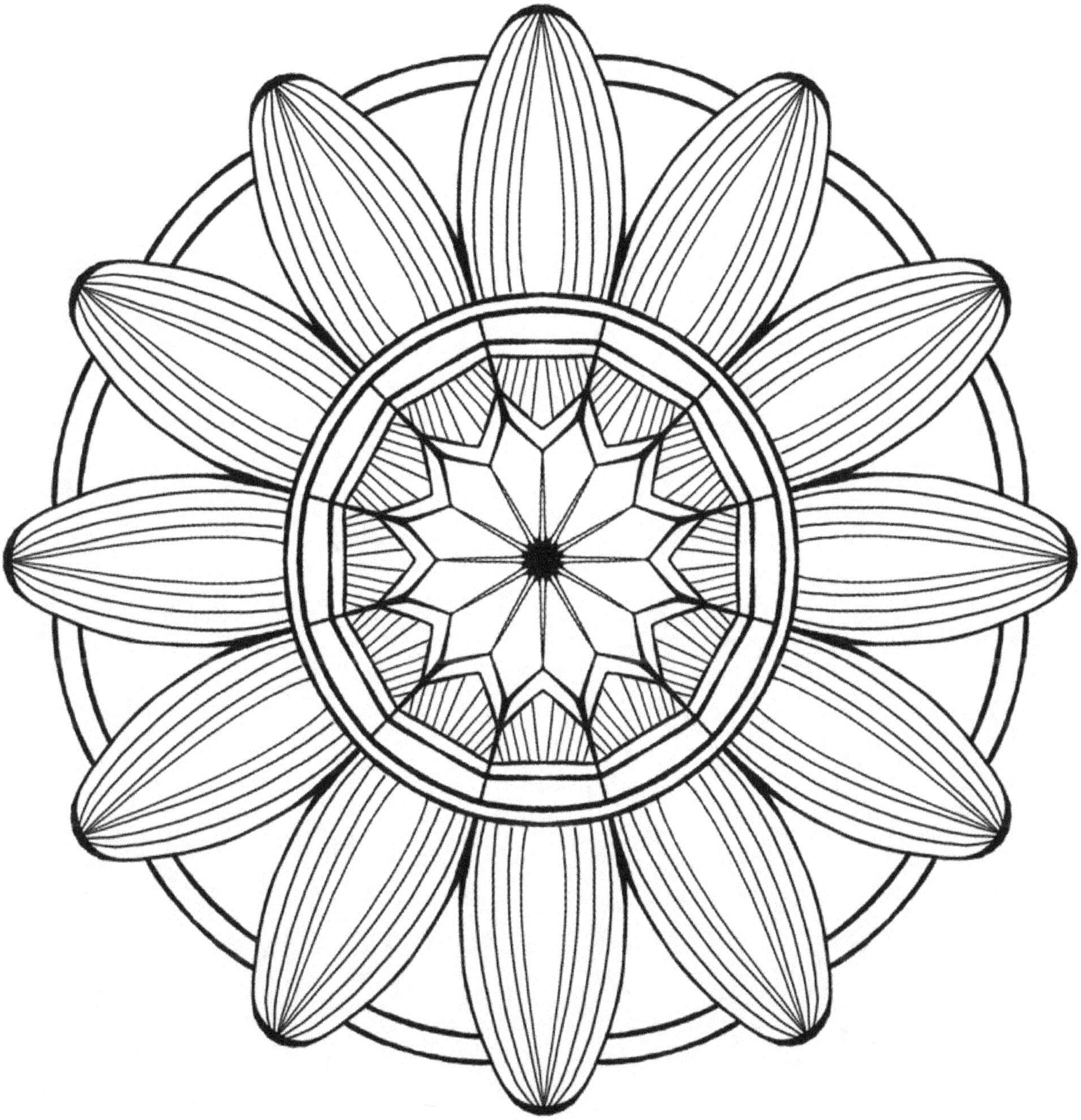

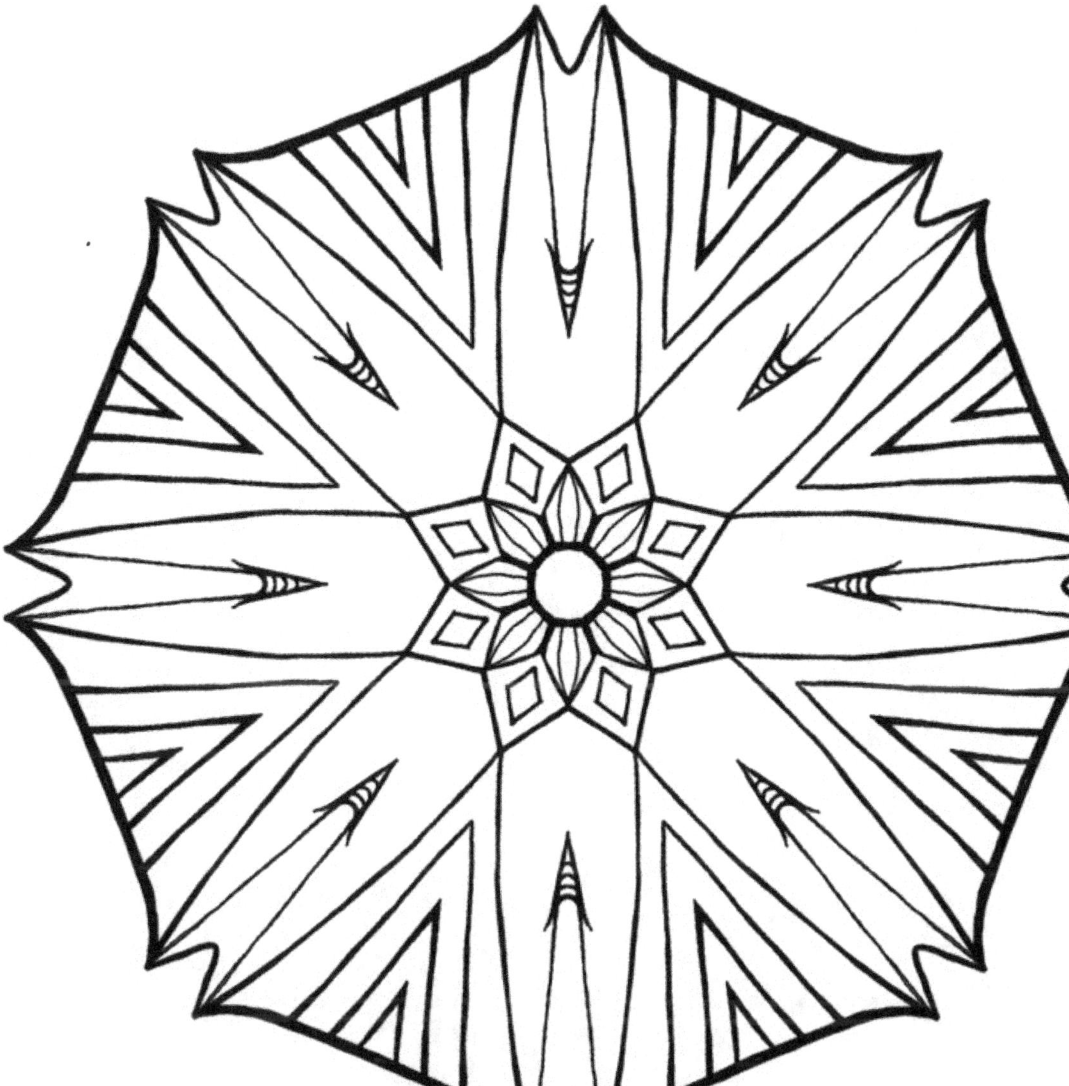

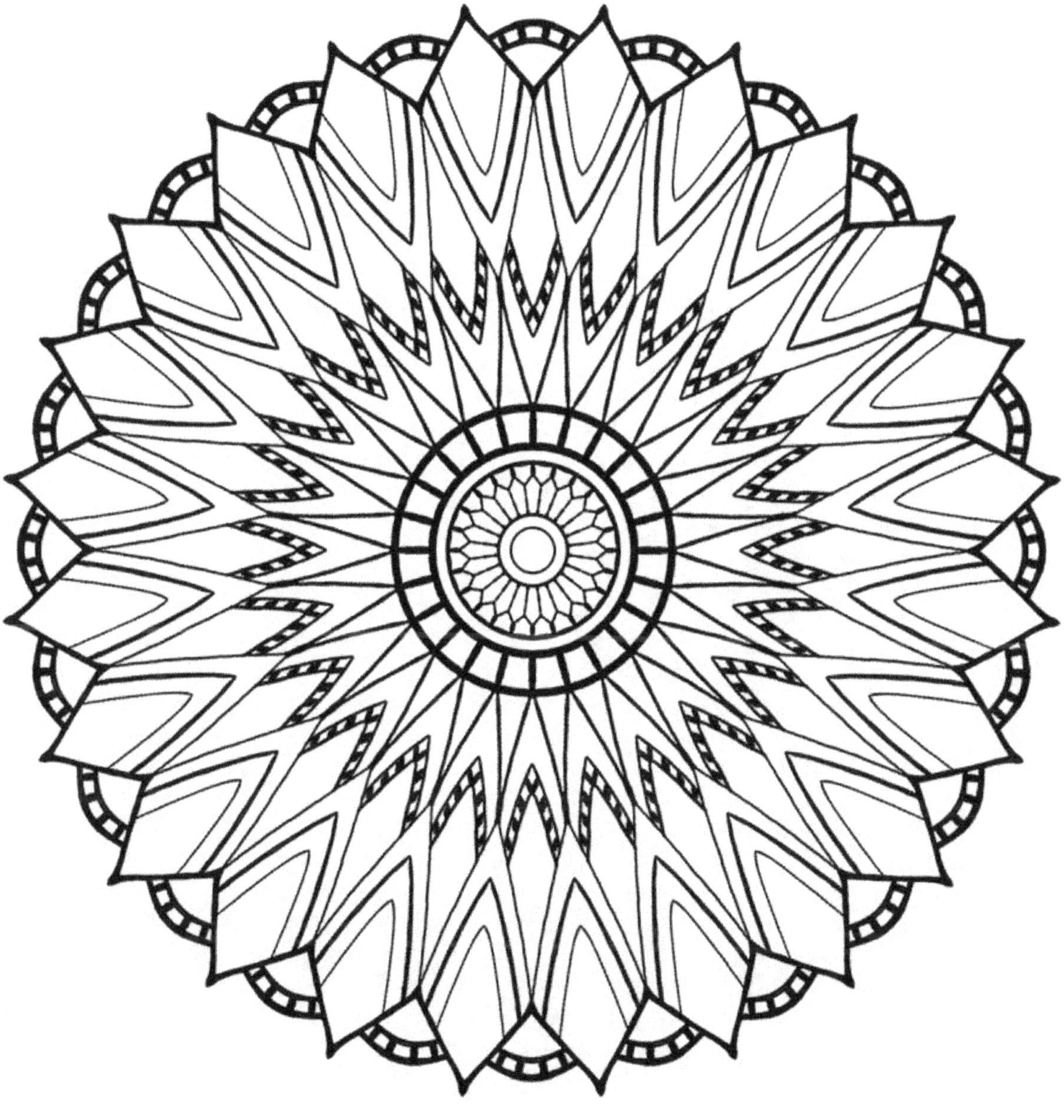

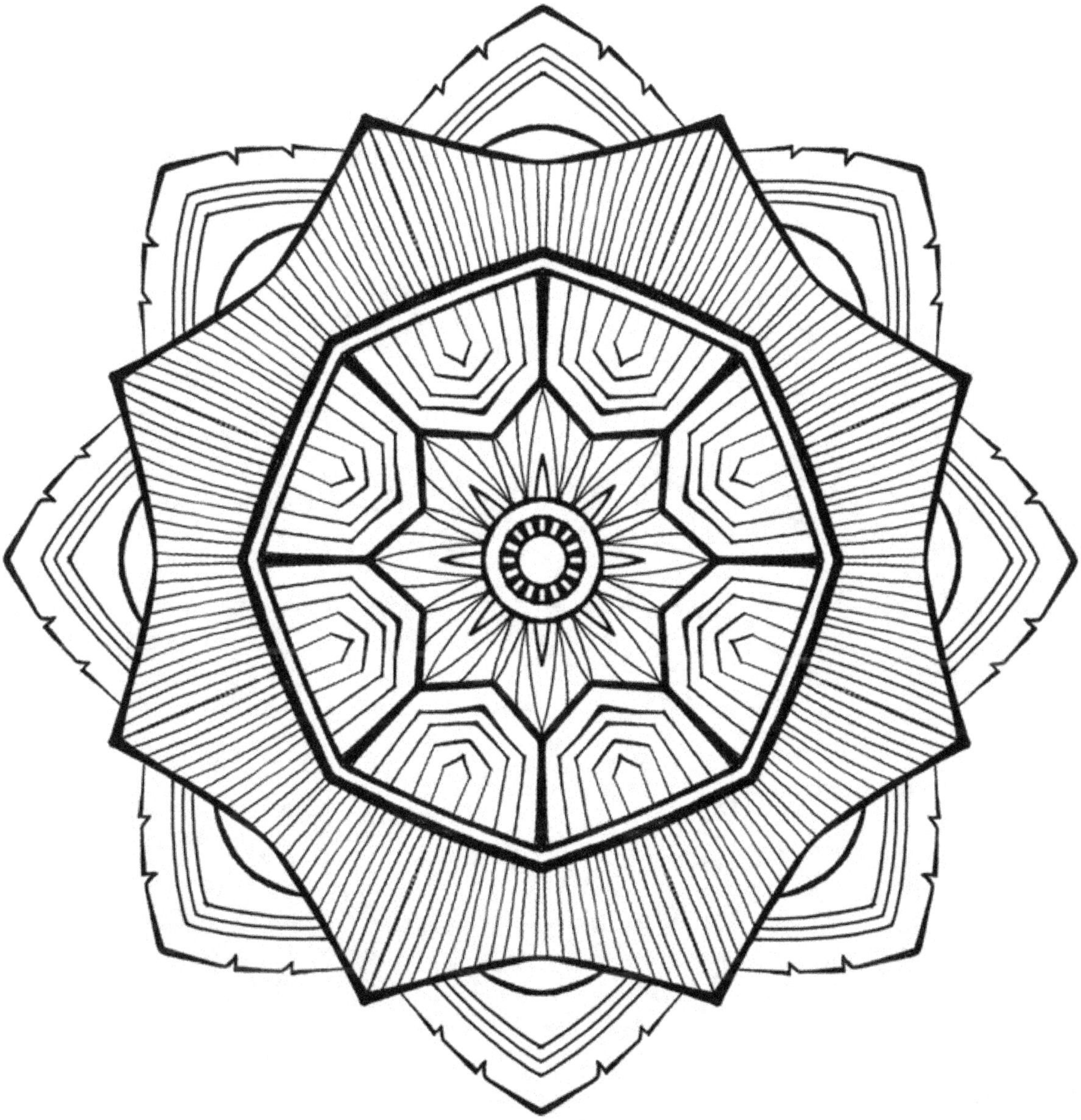

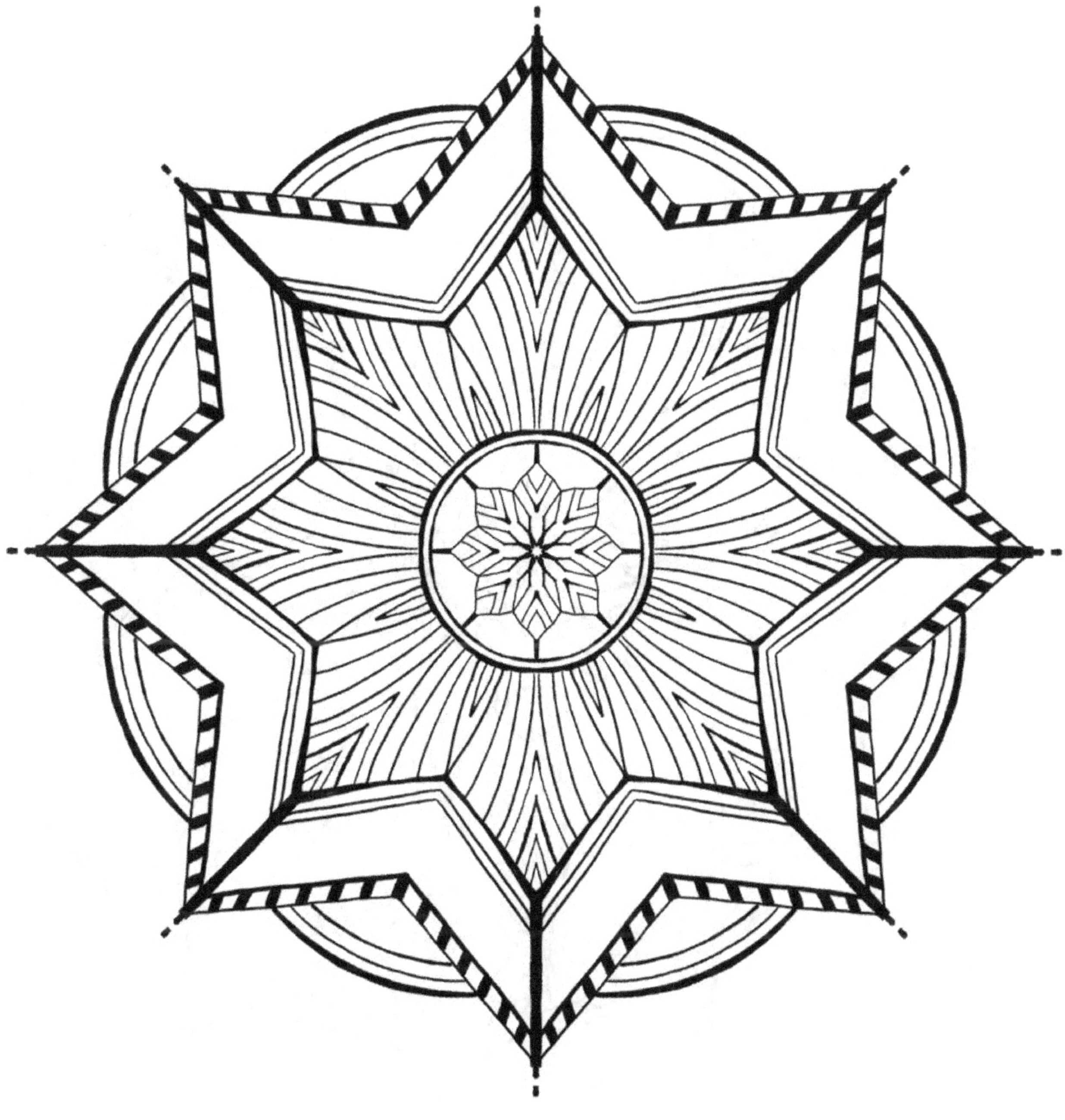

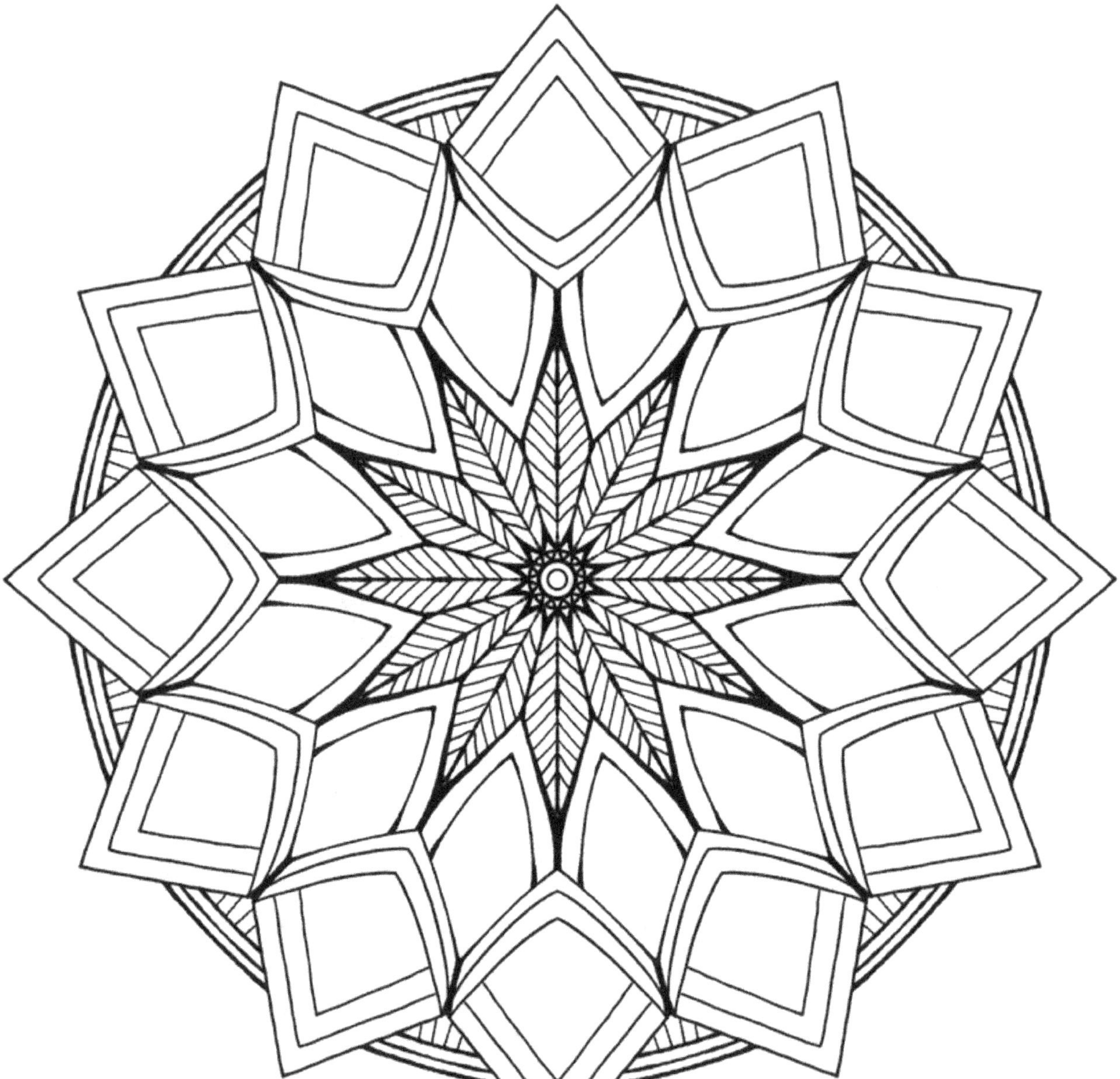

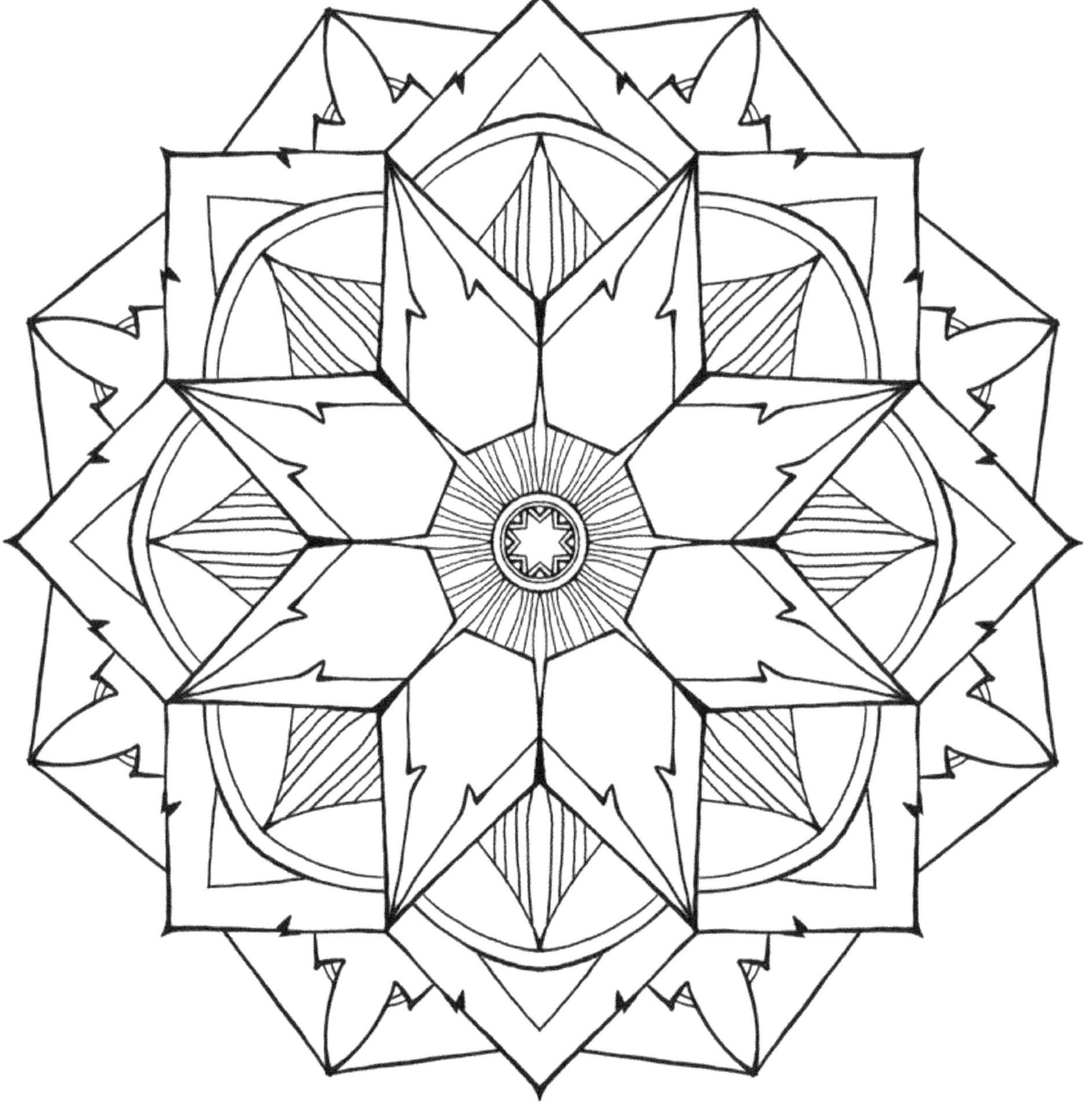

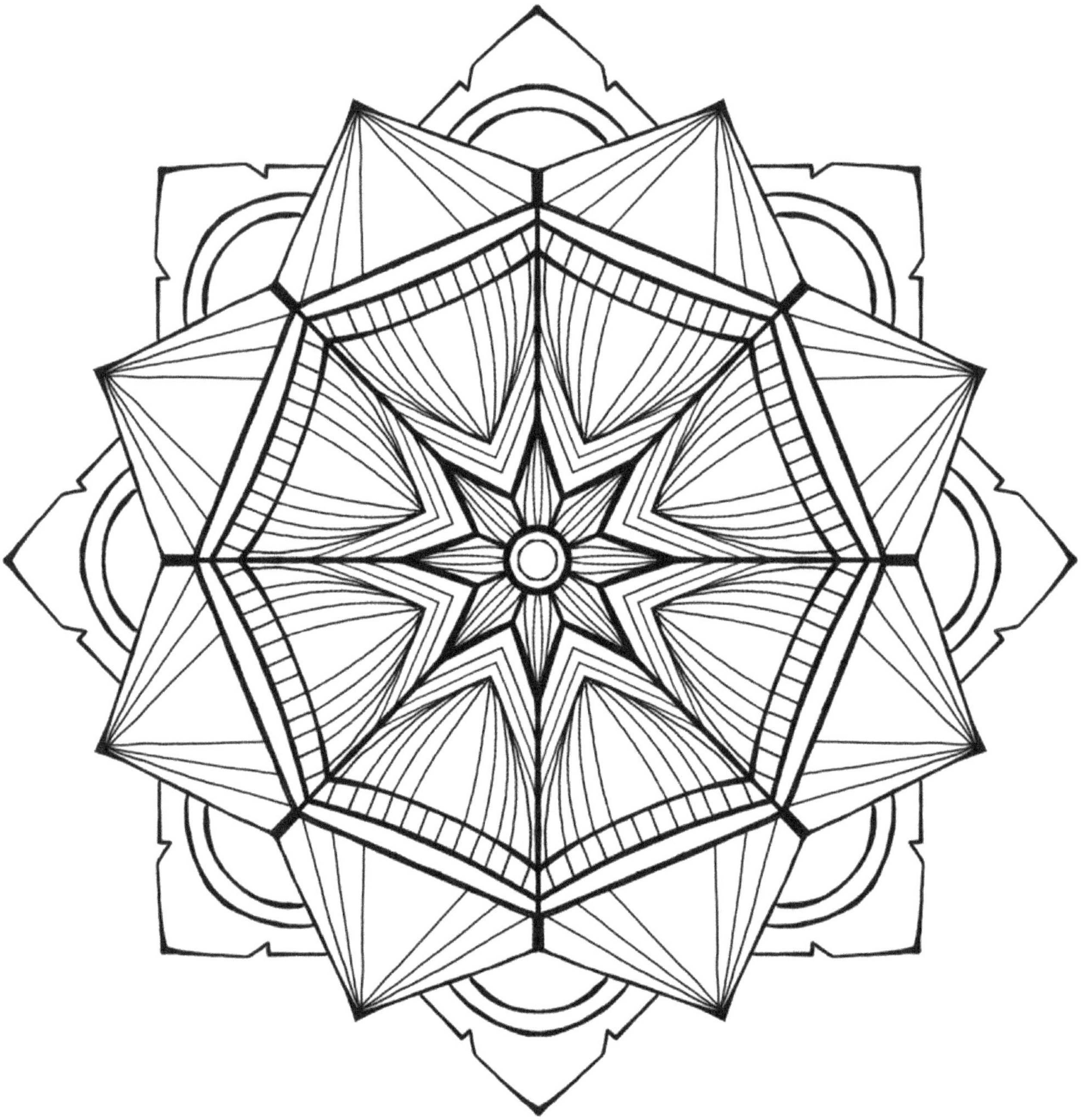

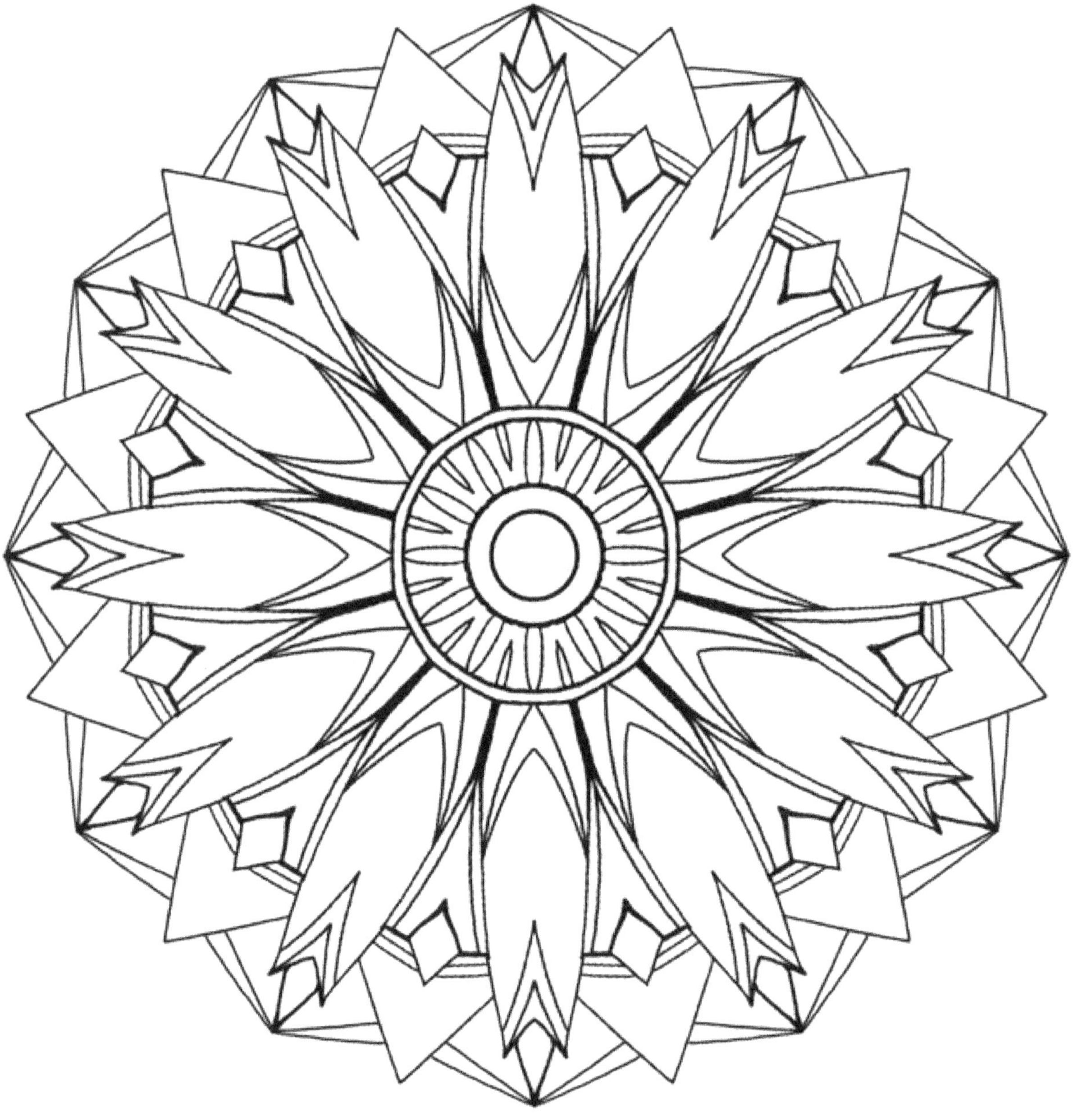

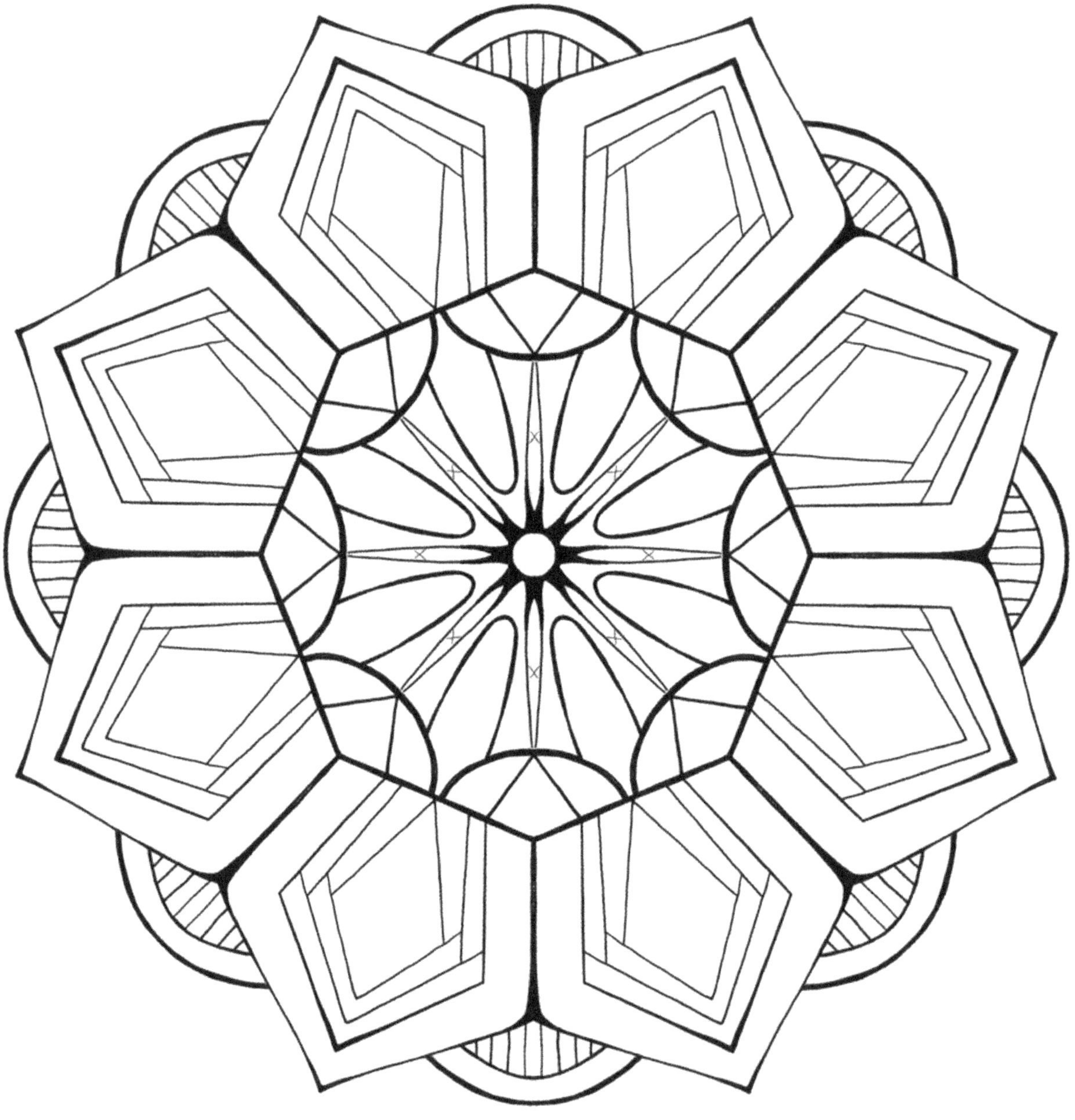

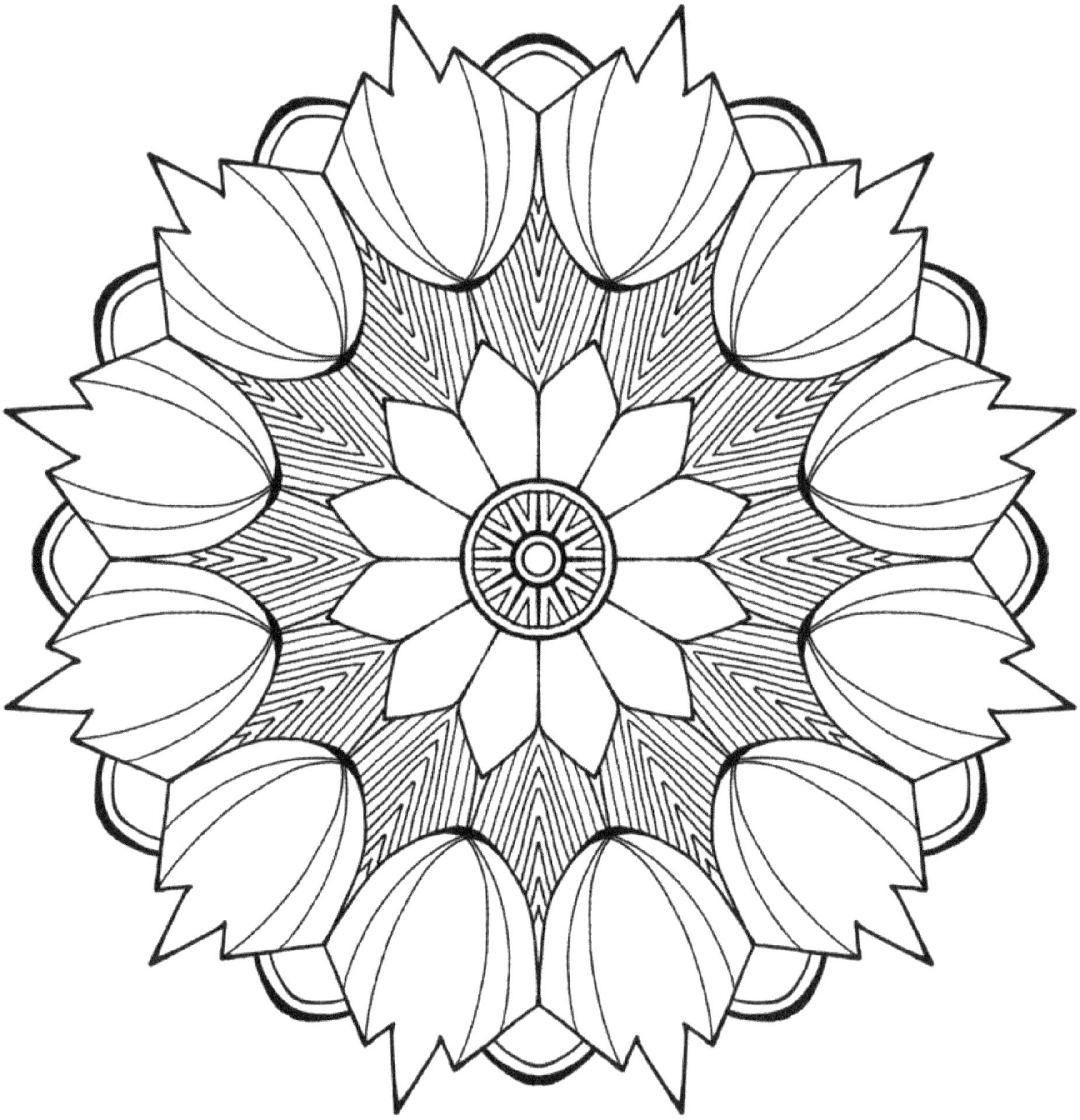

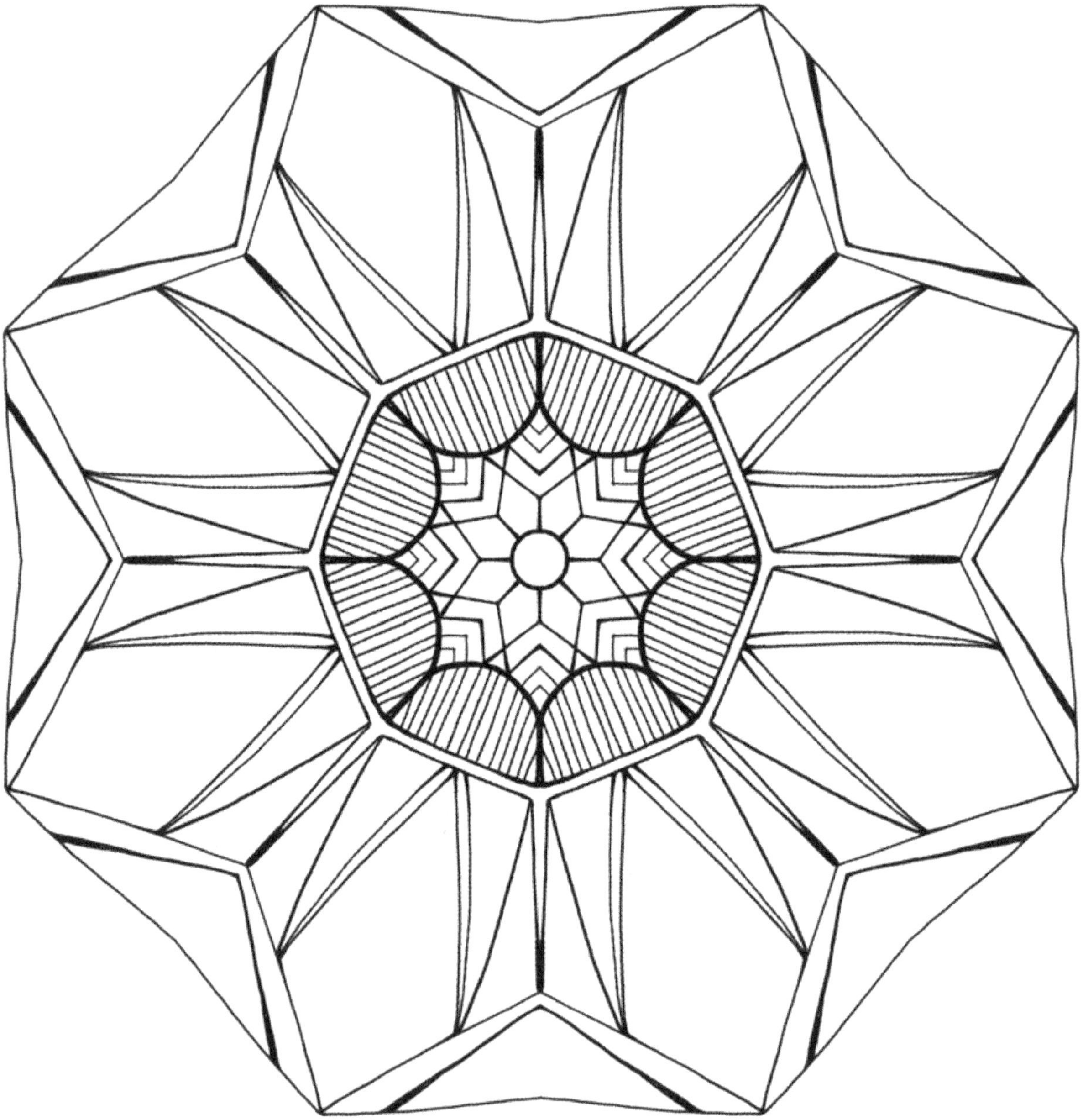

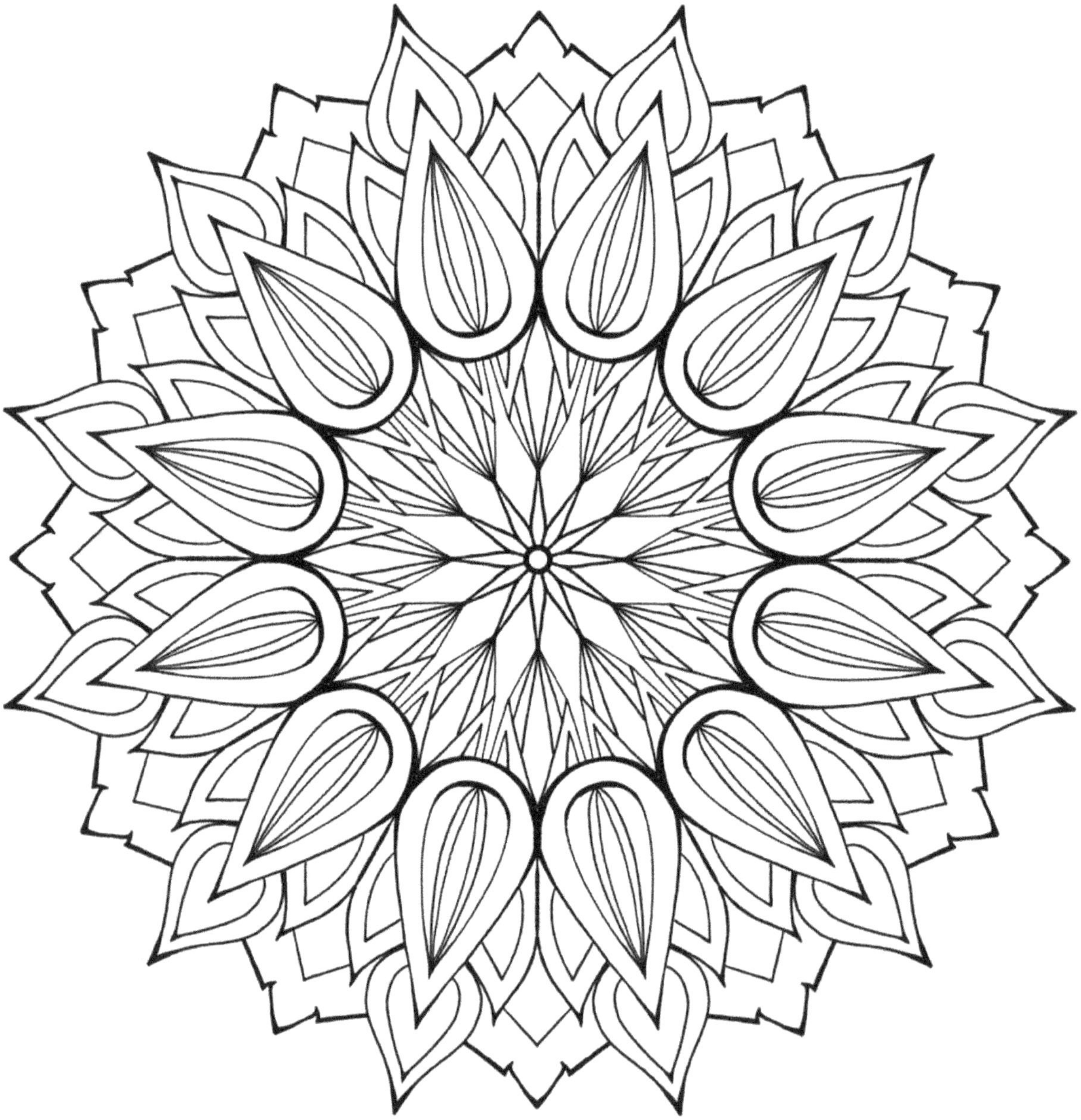

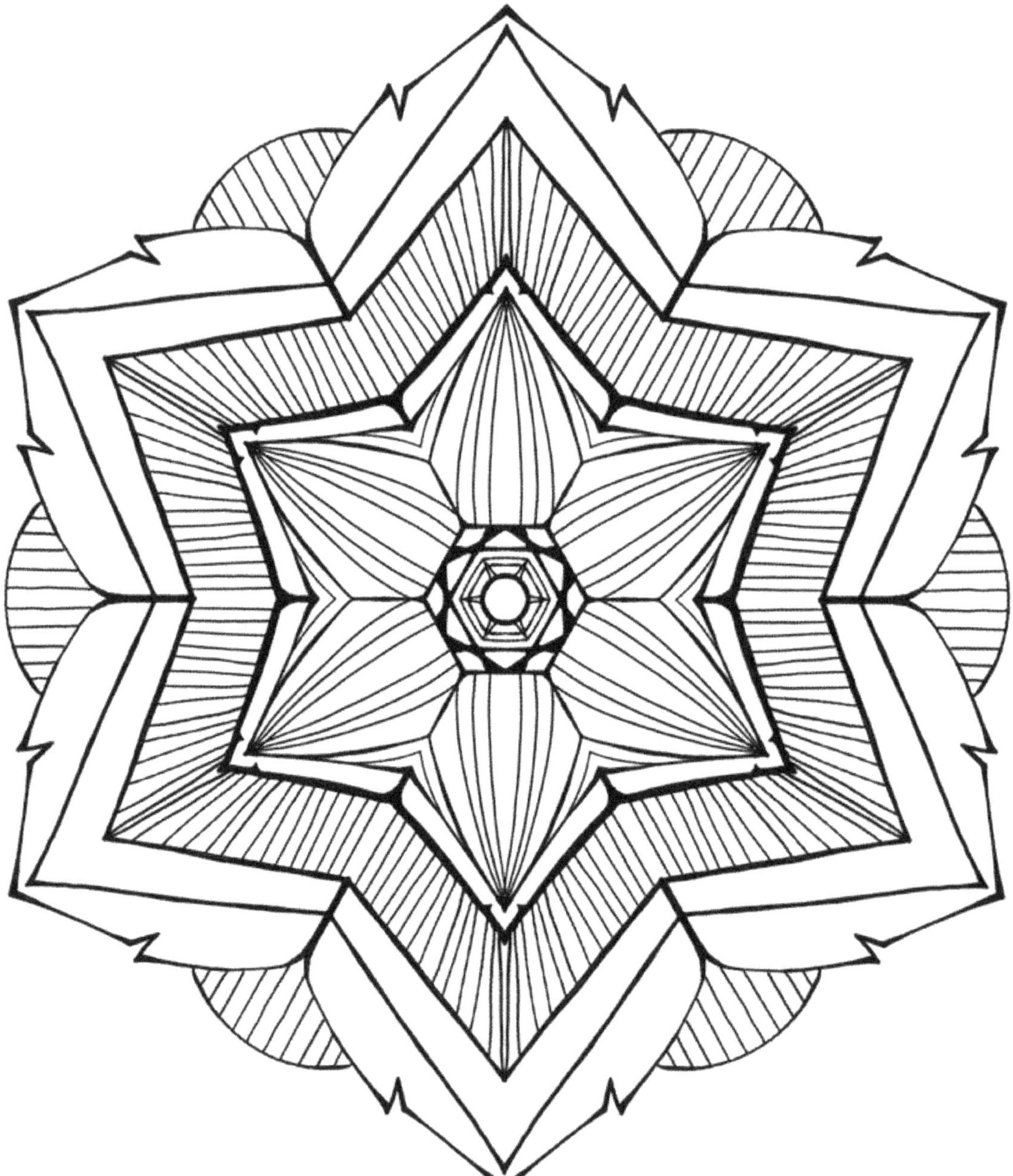

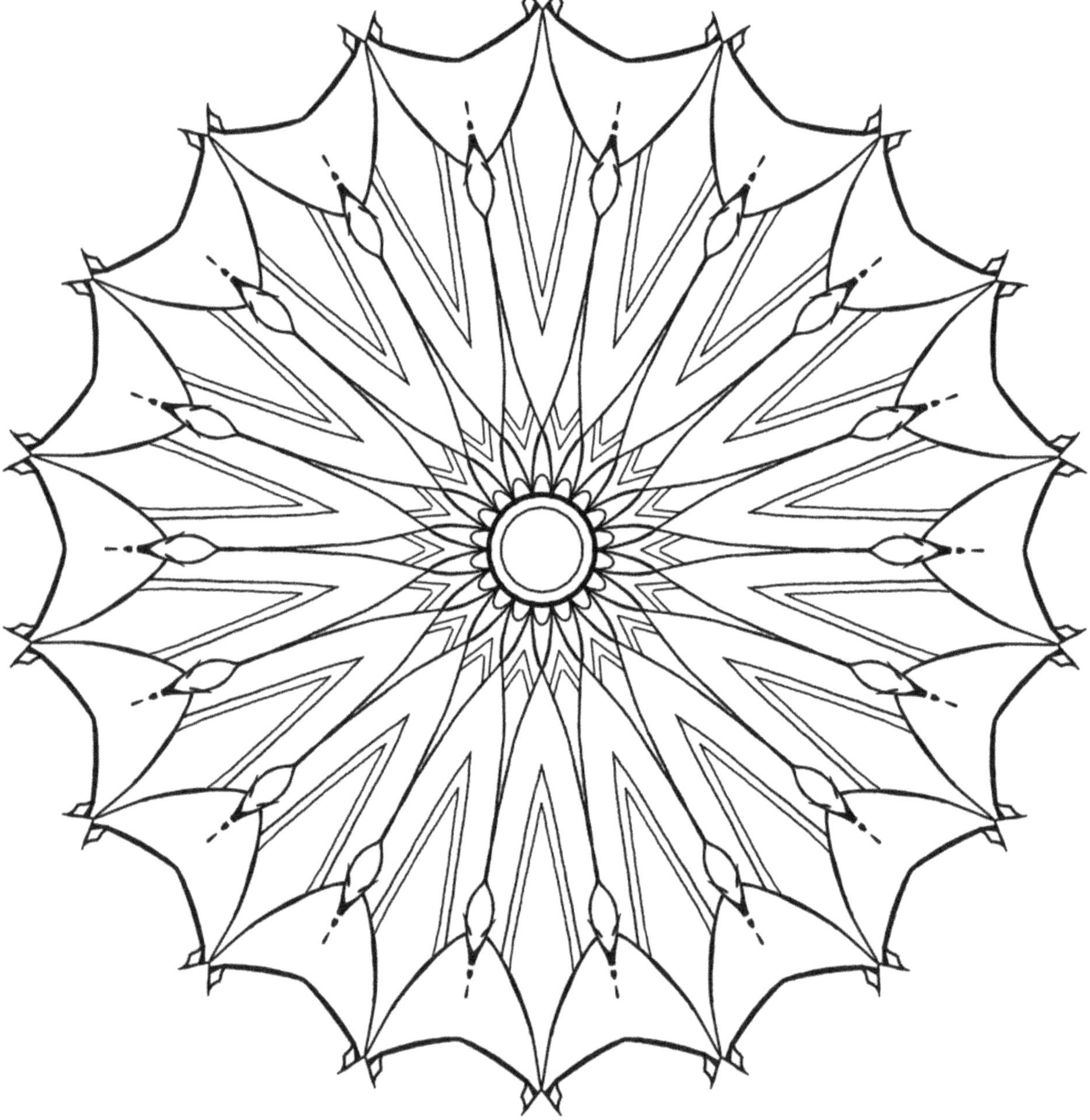

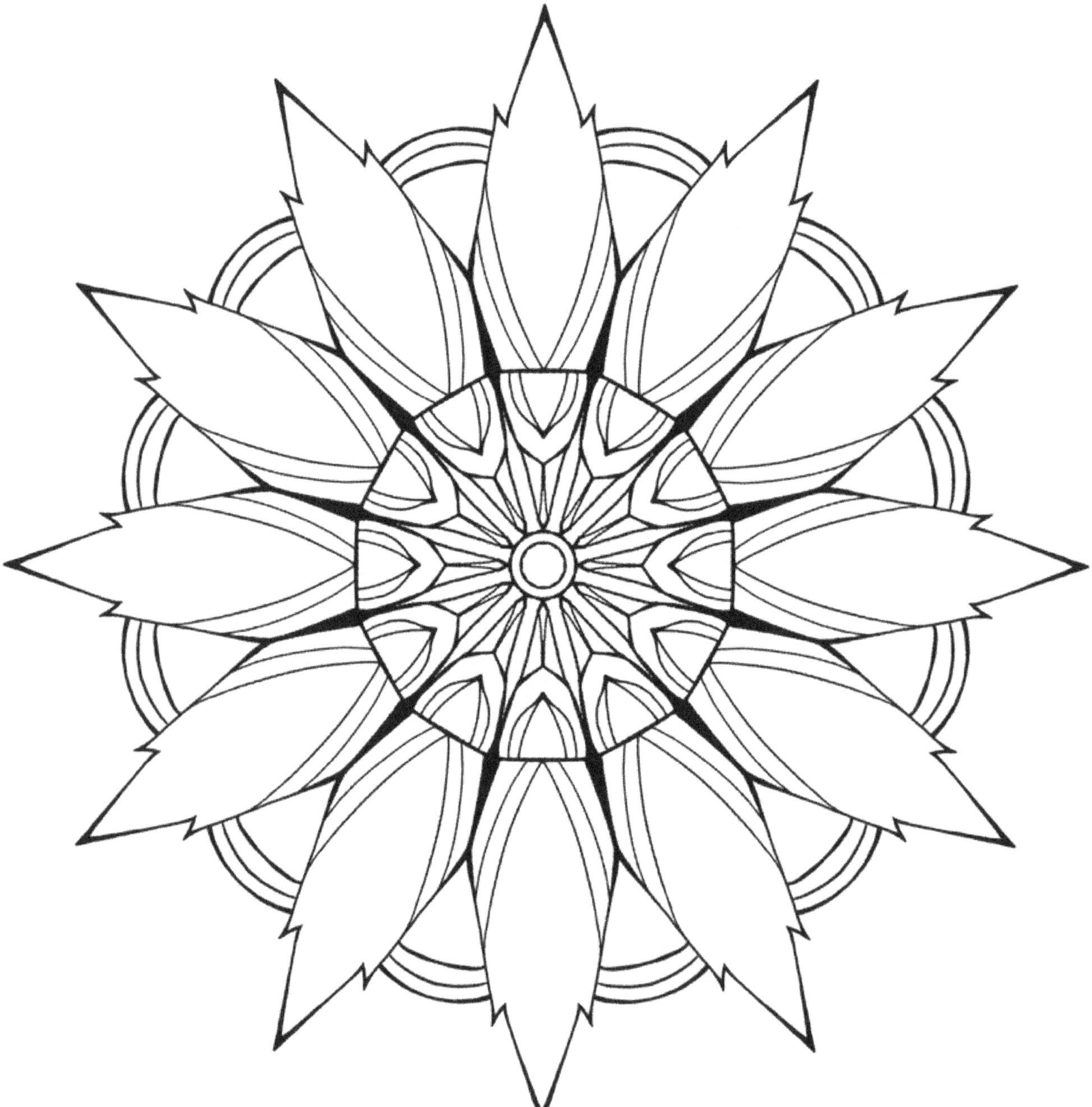

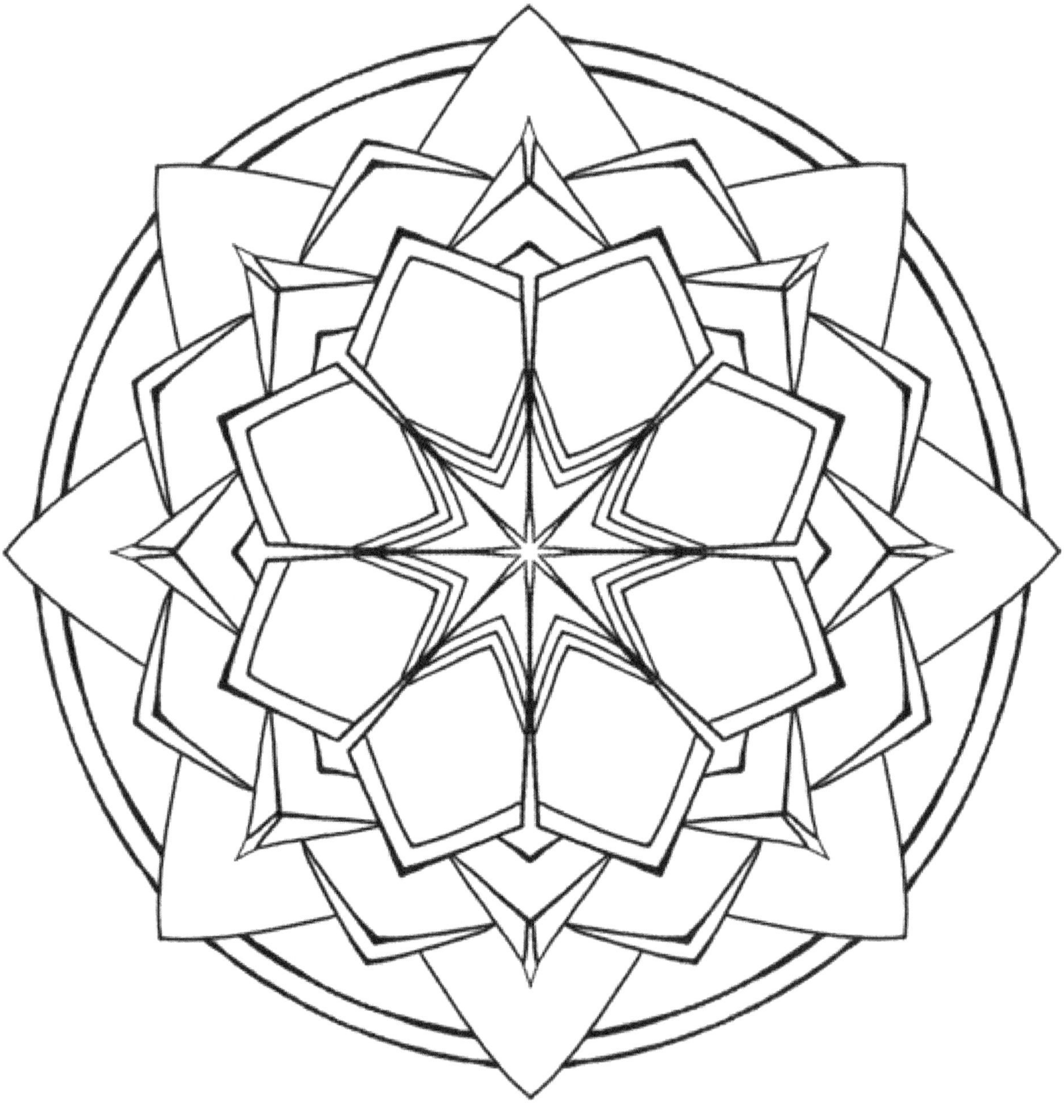

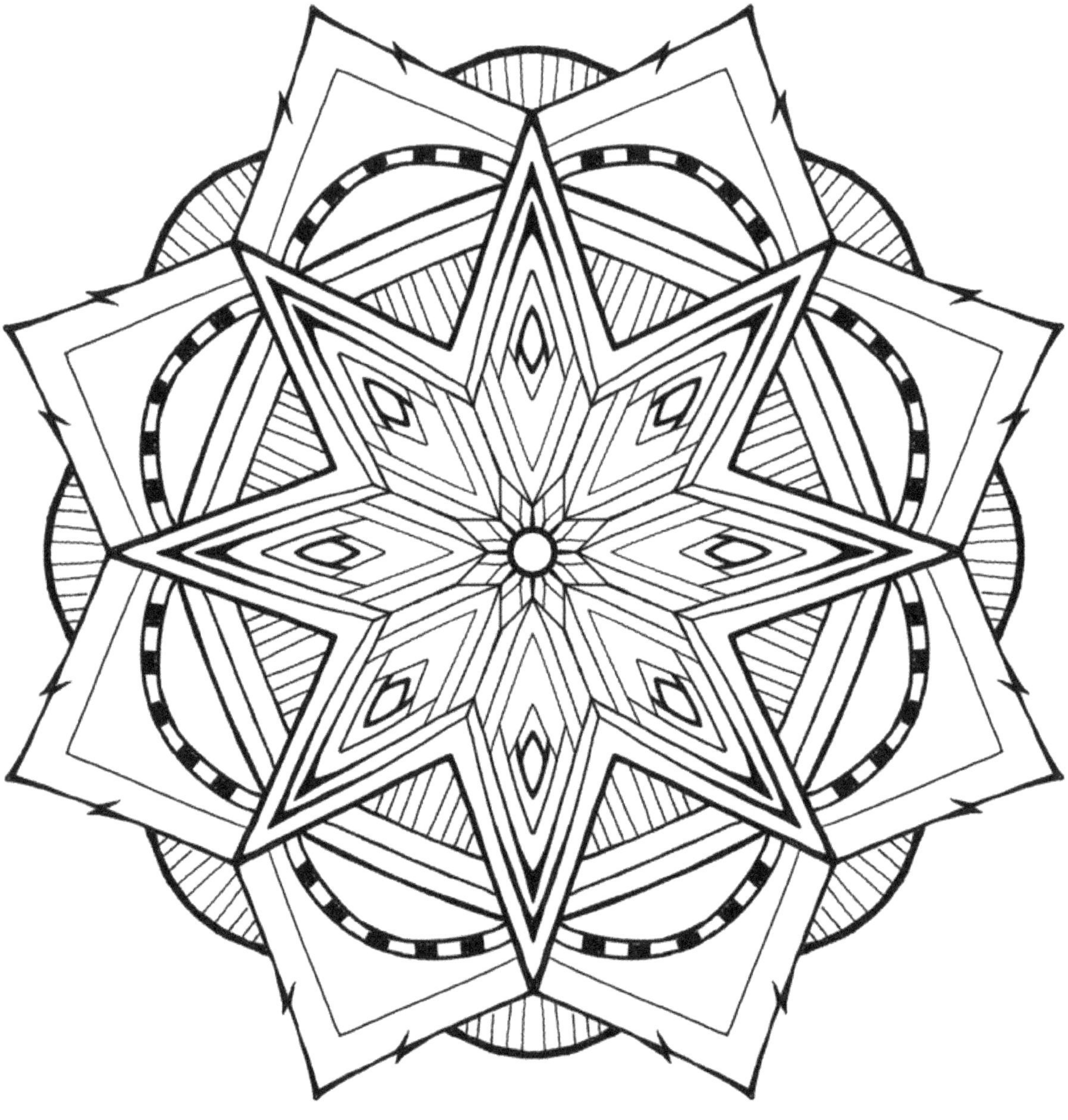

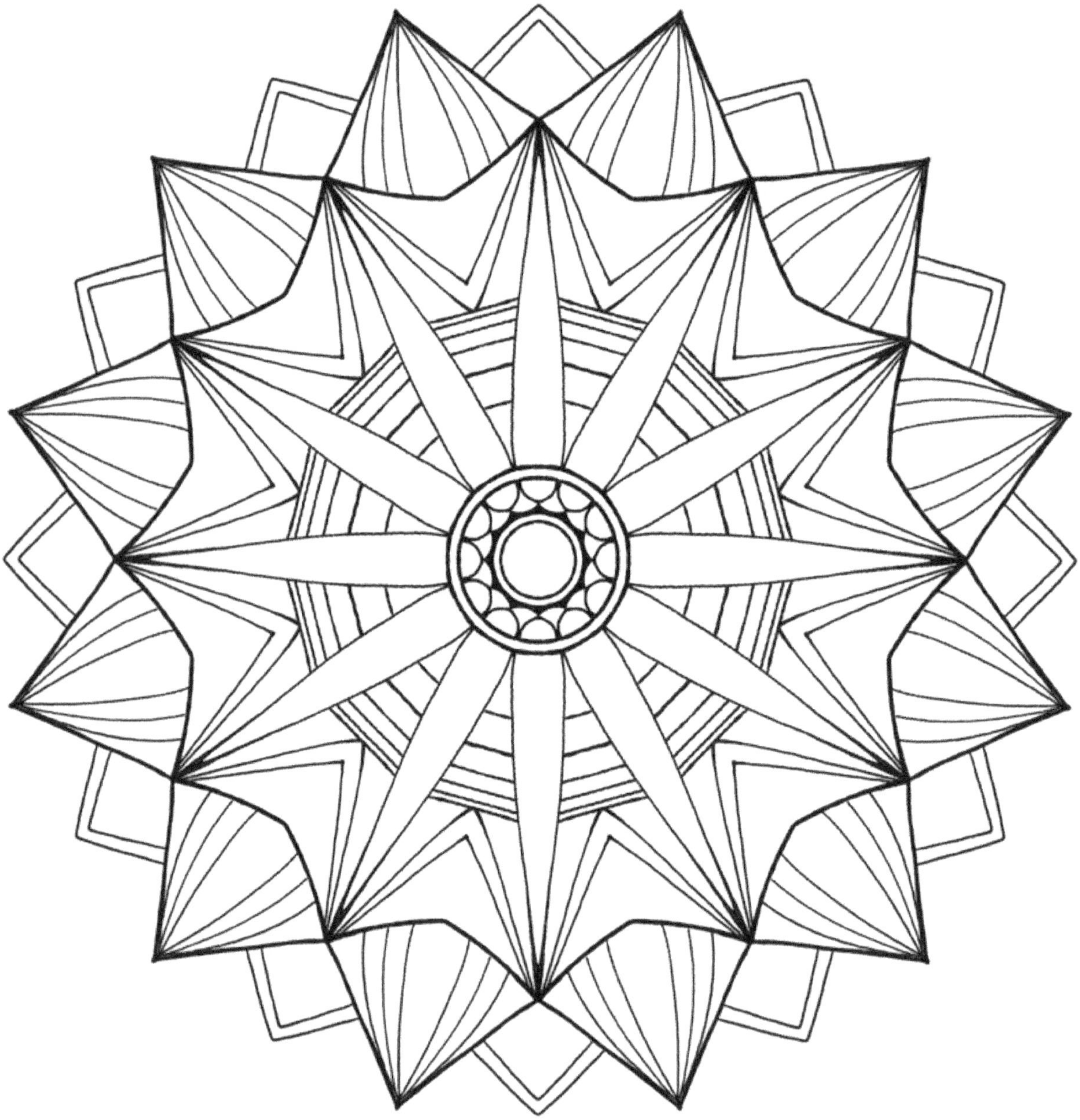

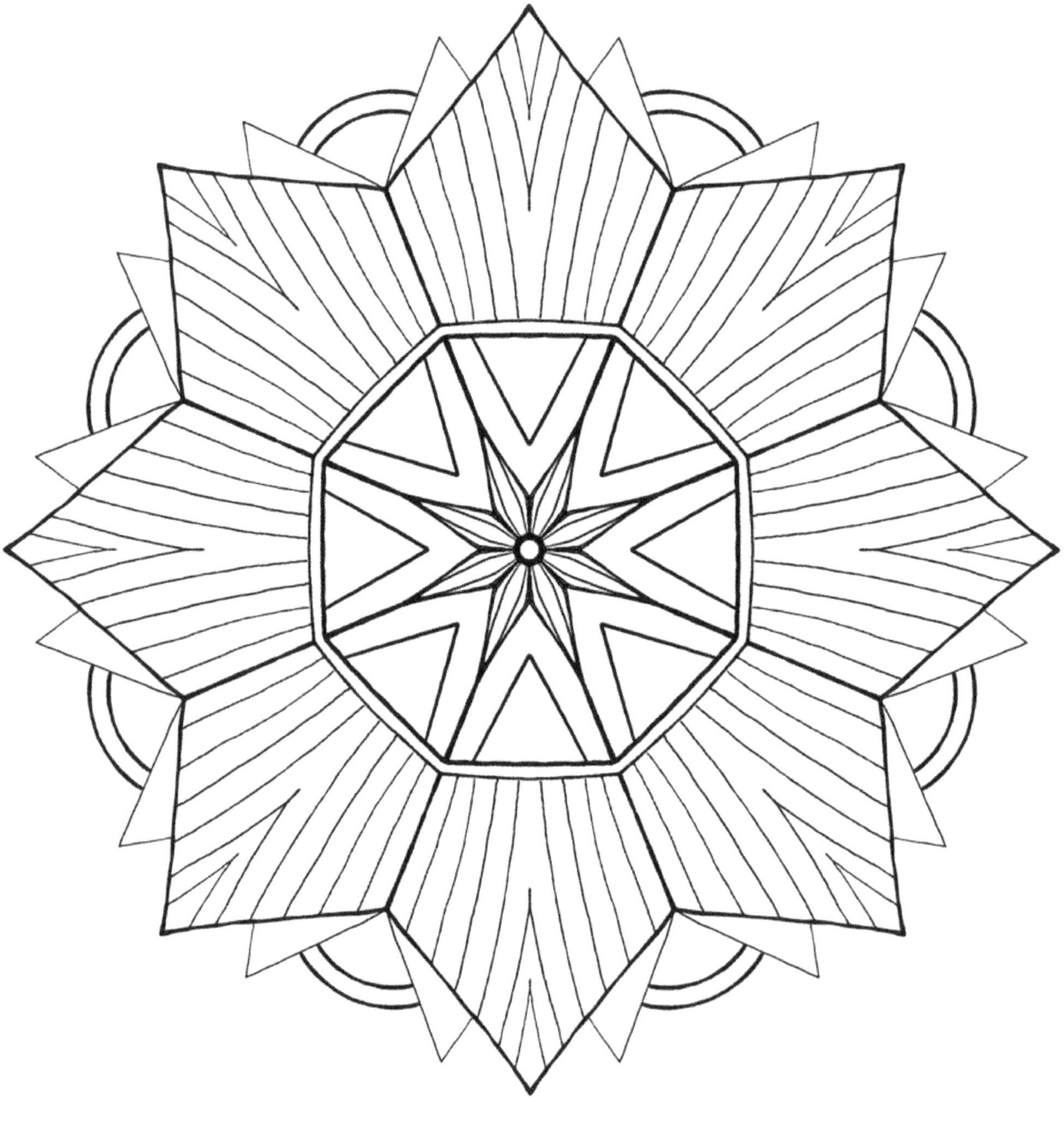

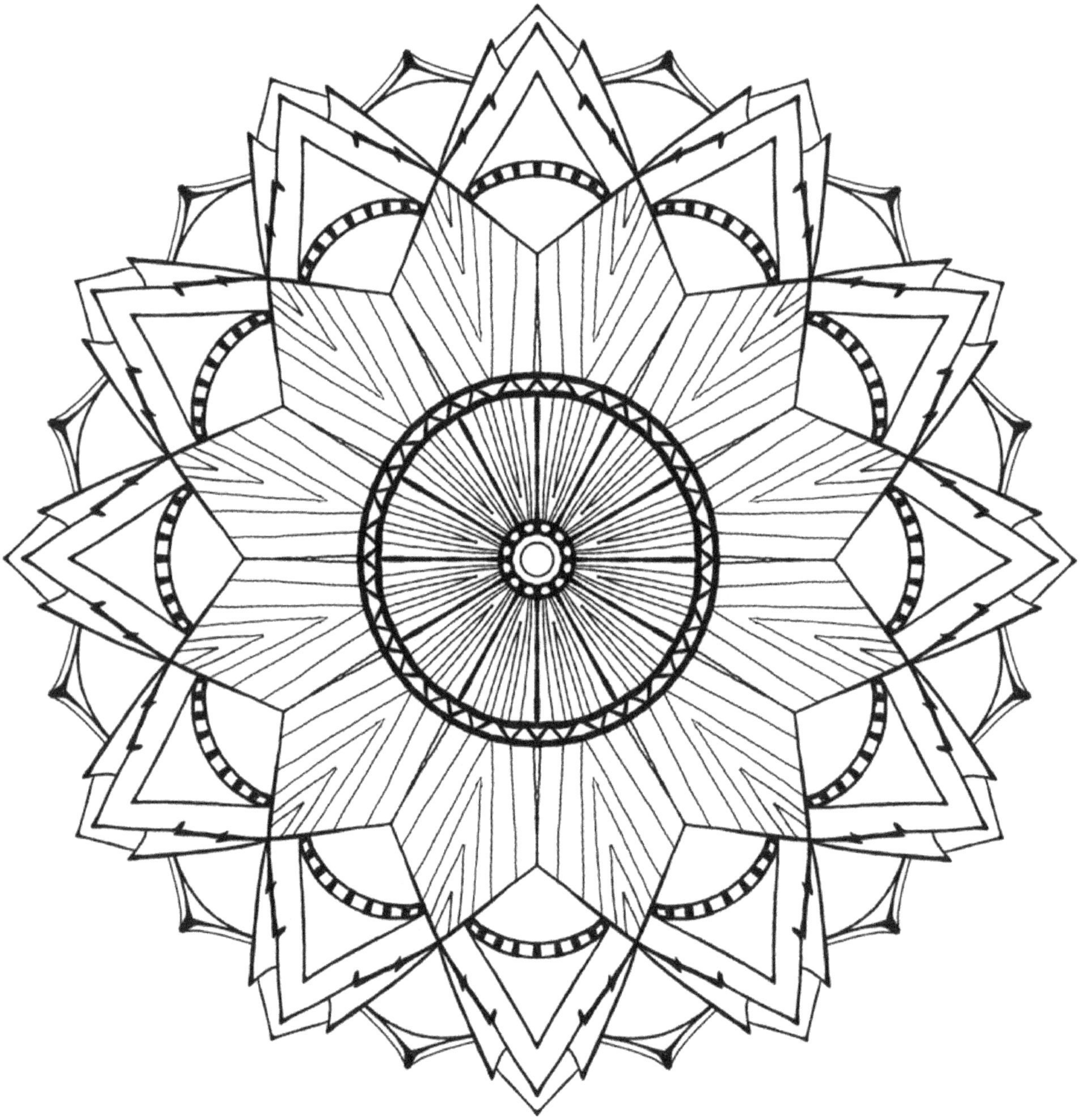

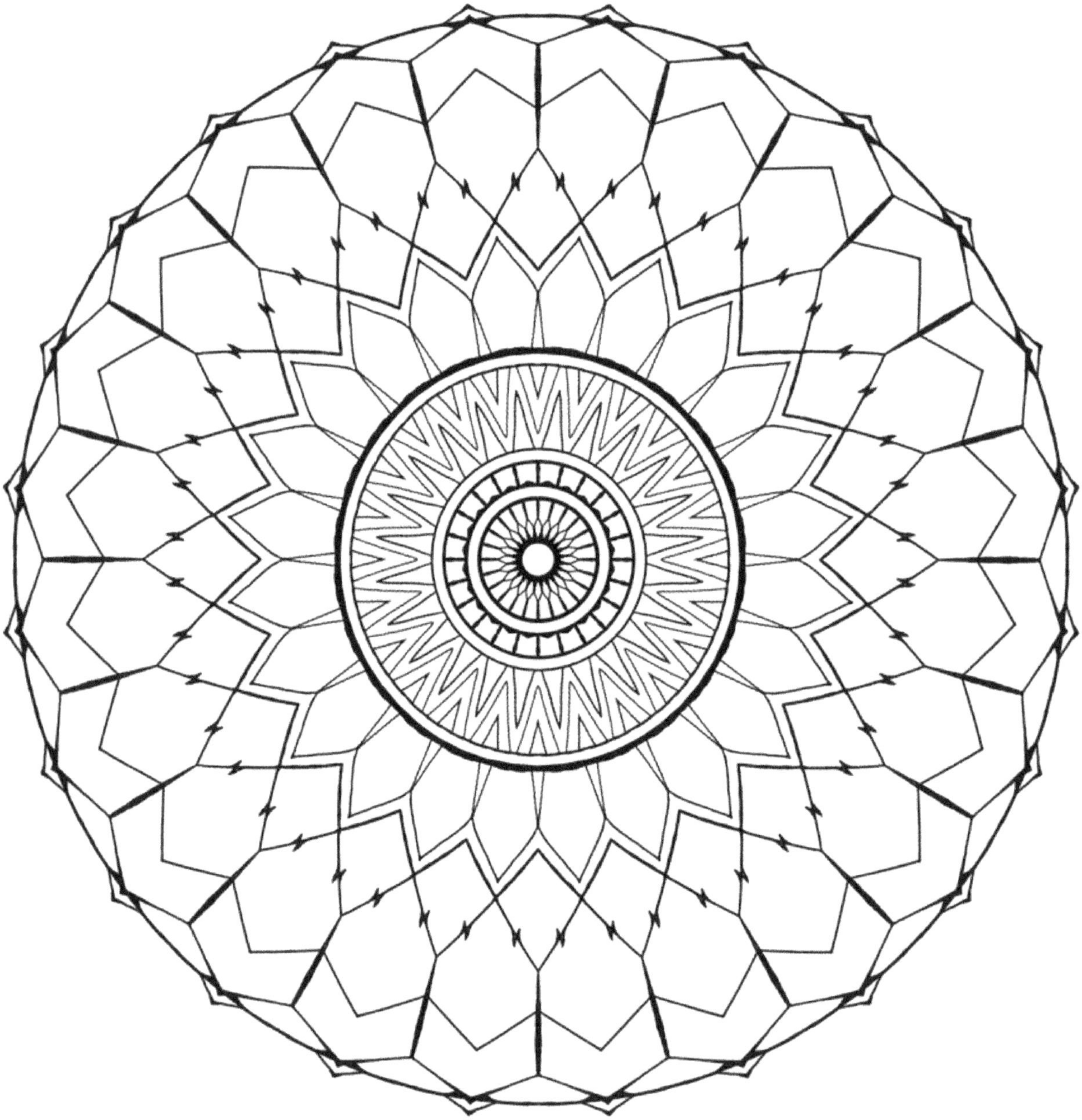

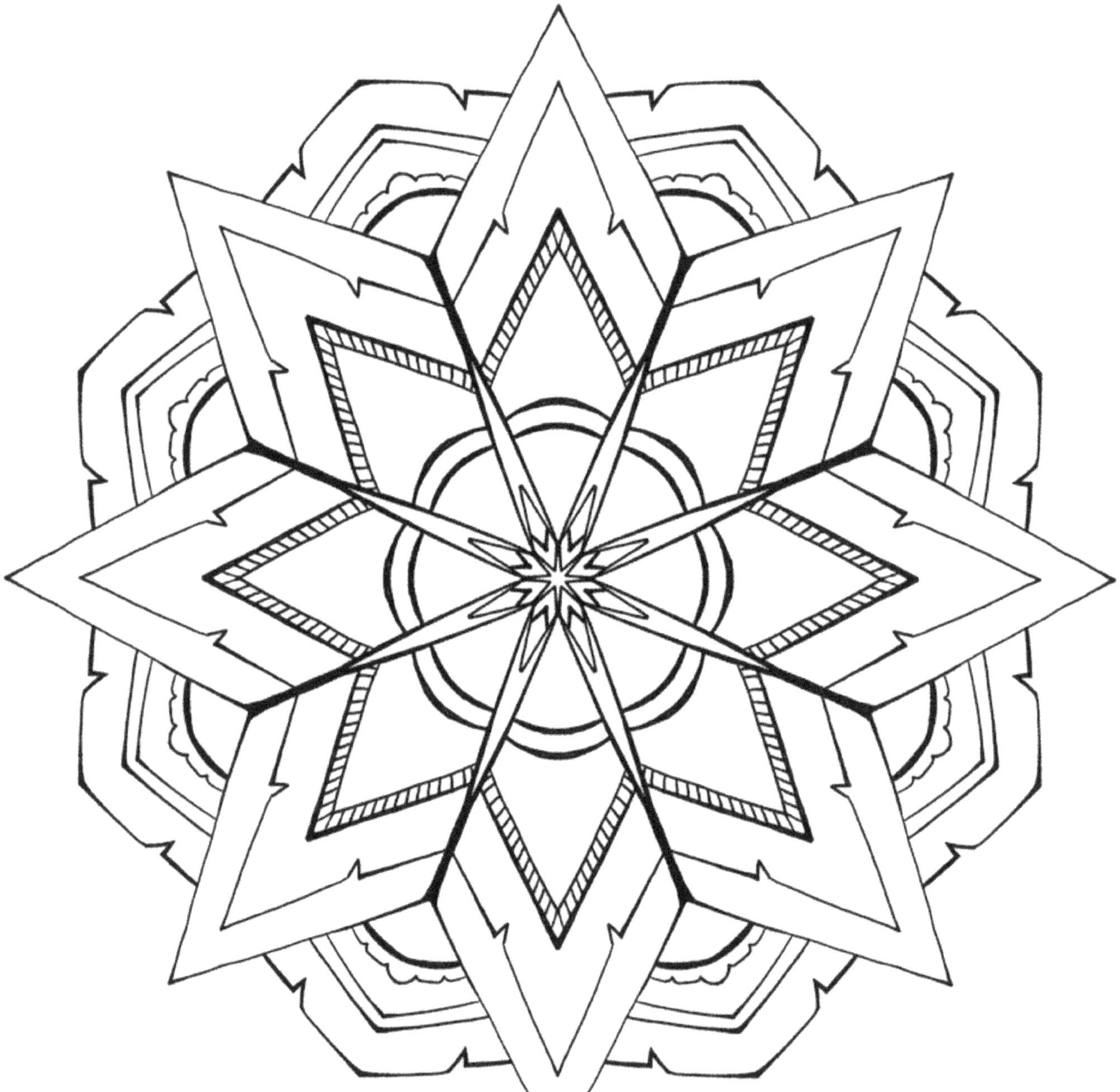

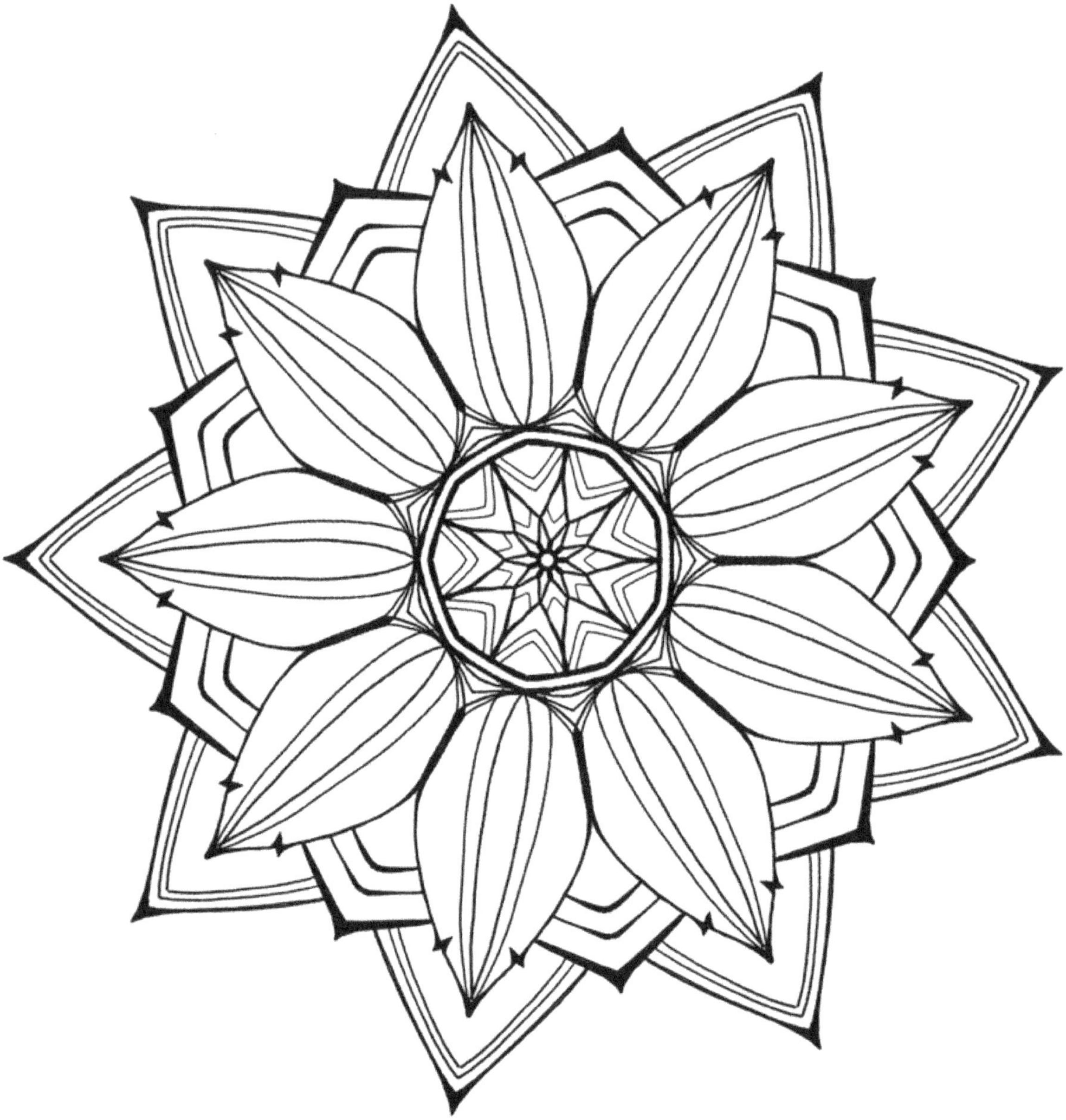

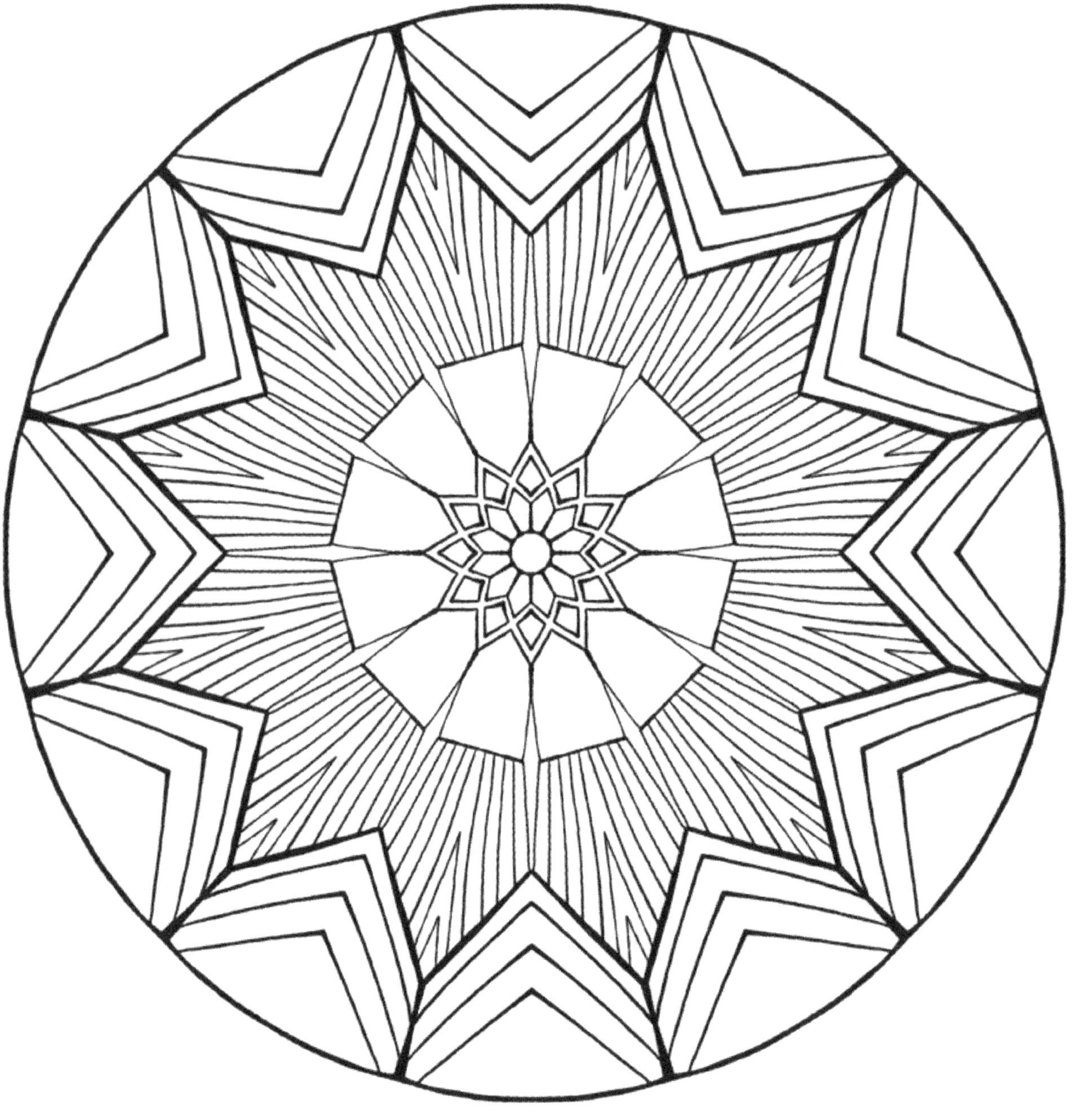

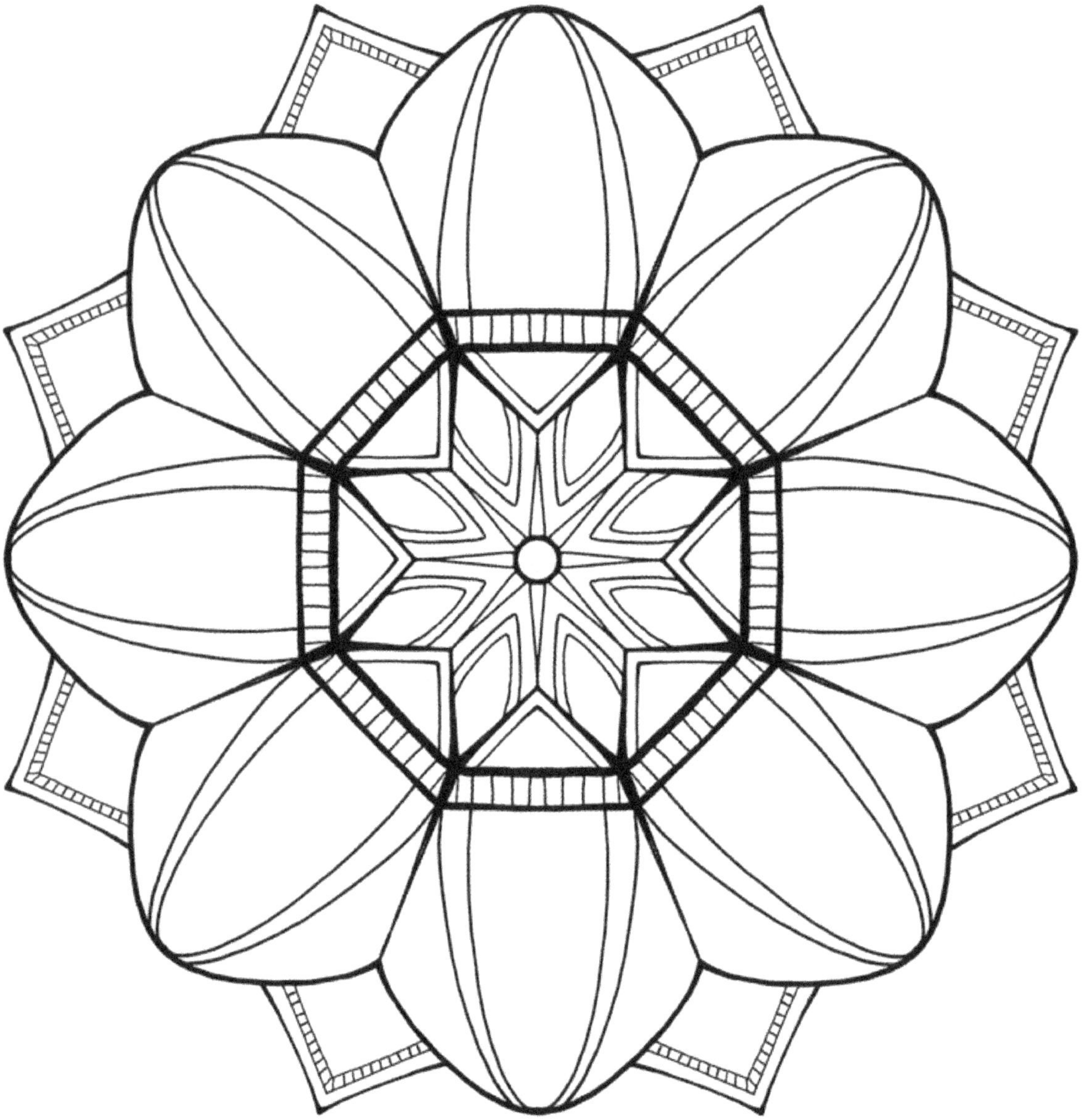

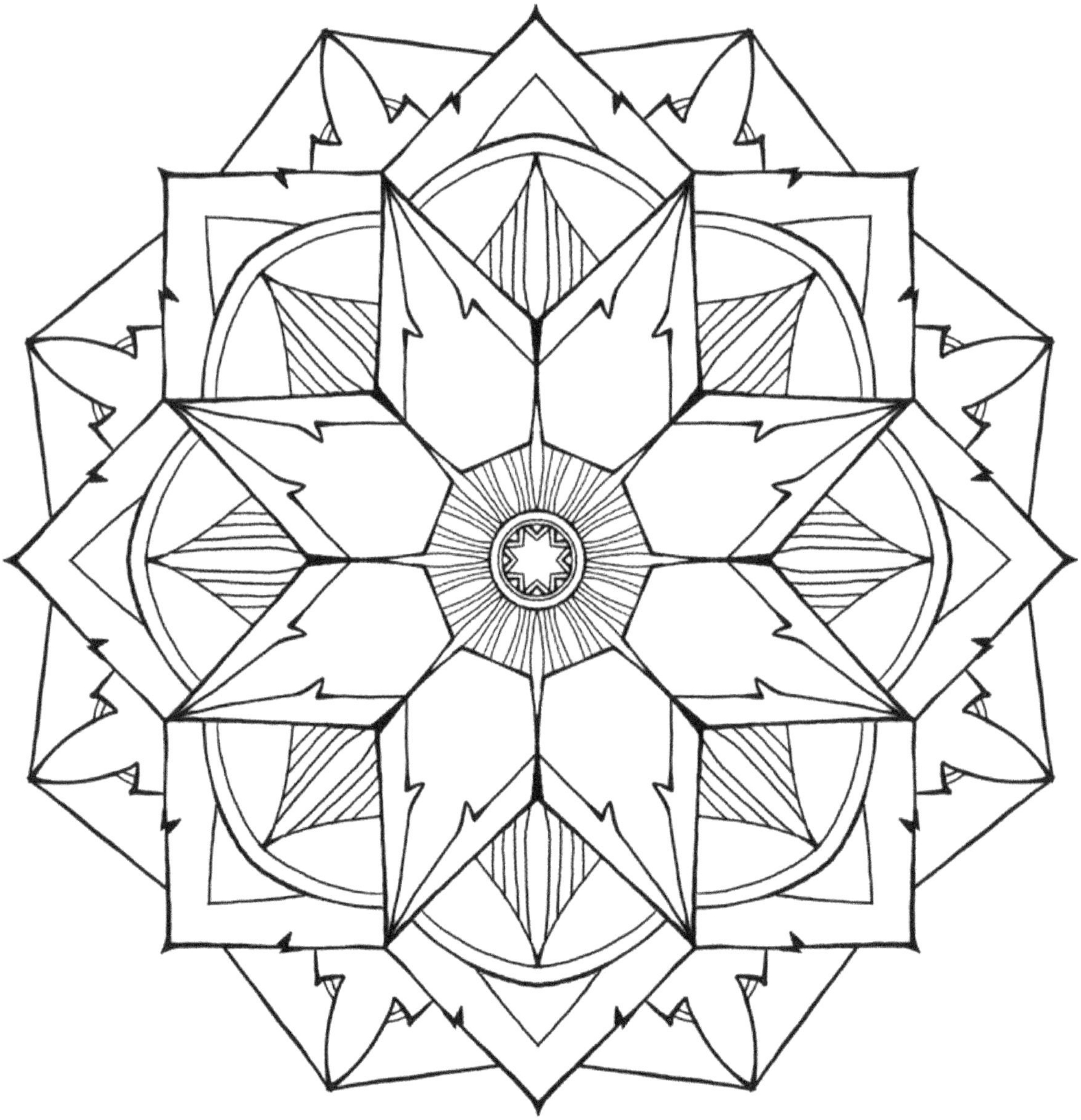

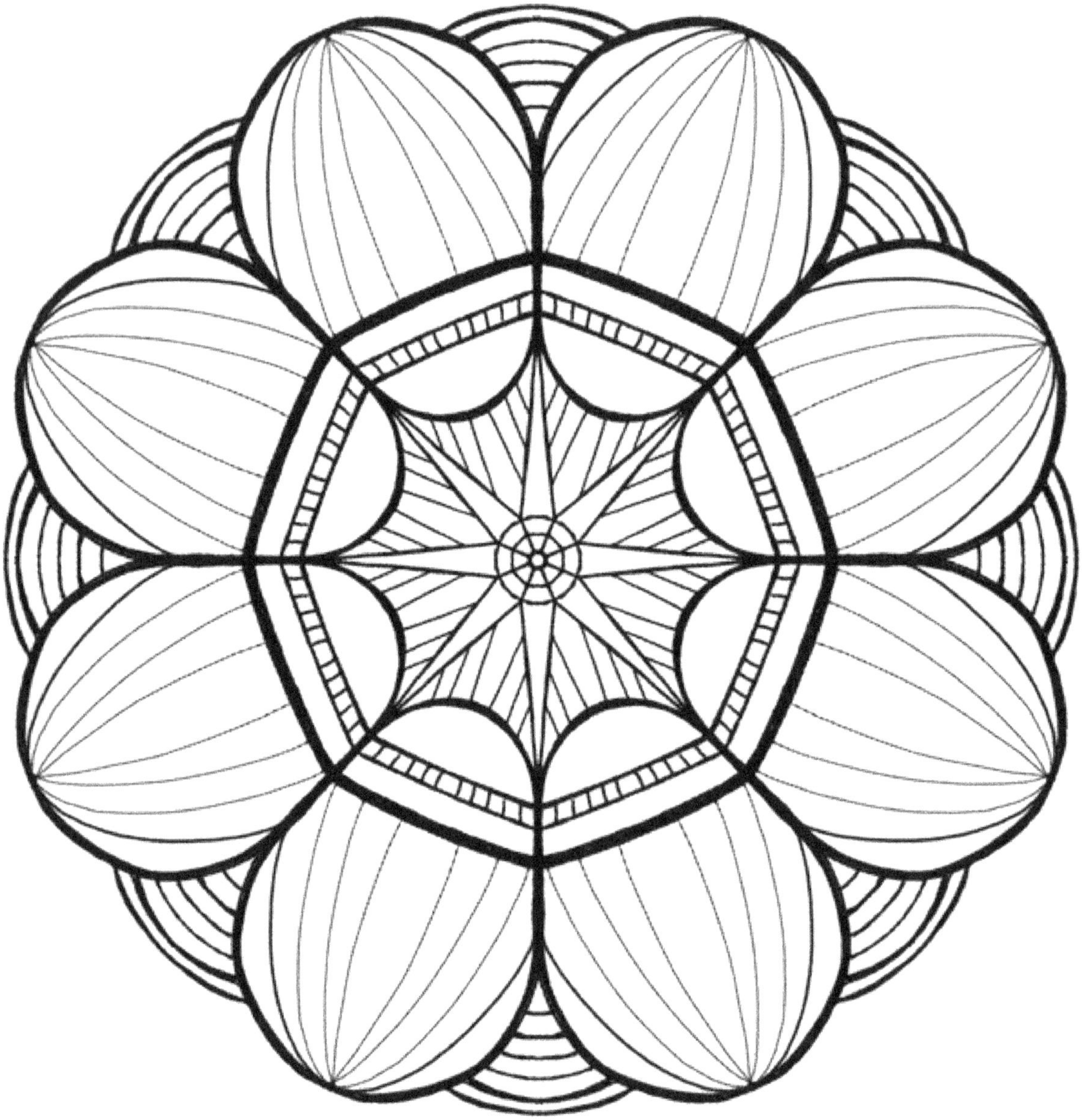

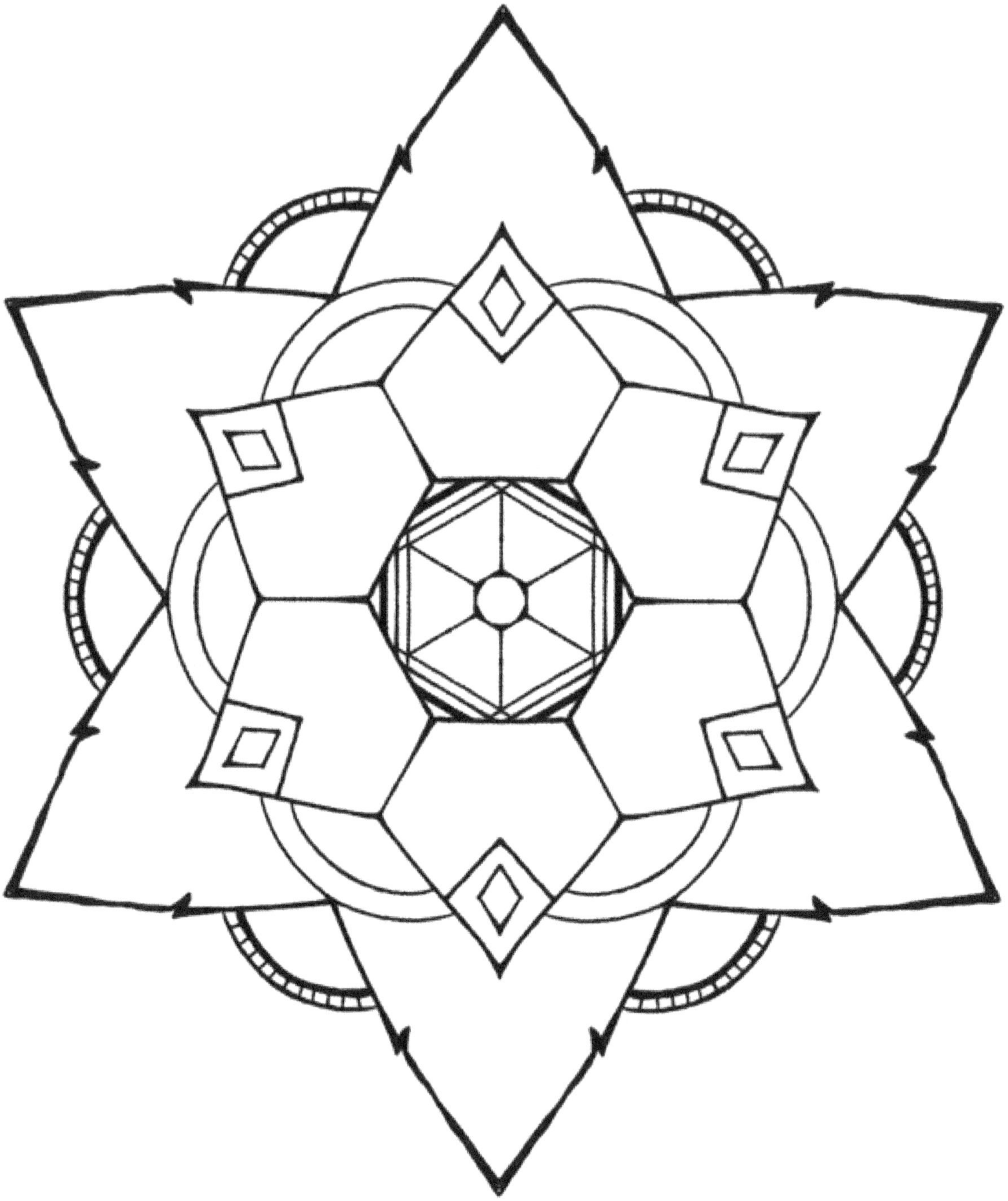

Color Test Page

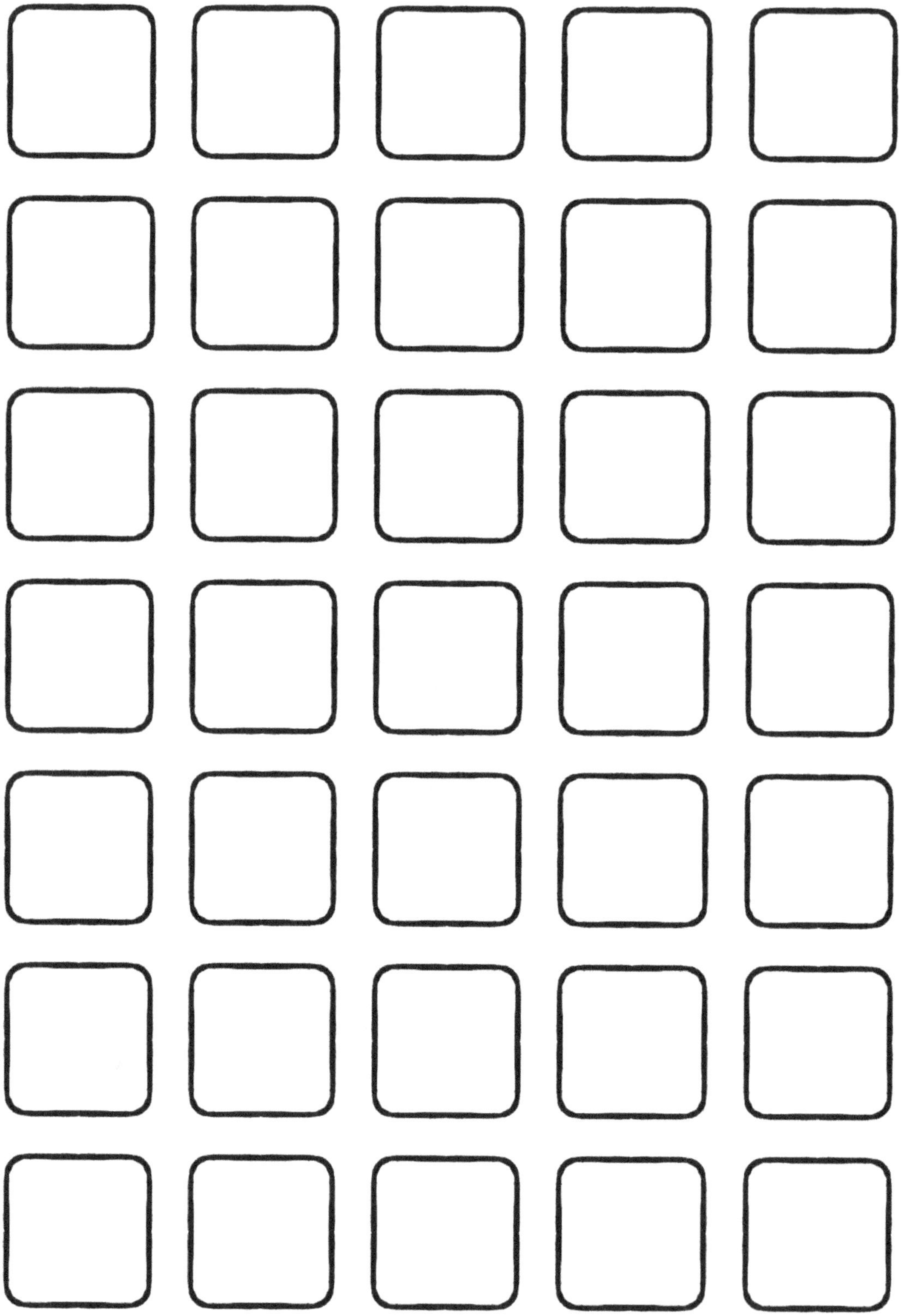

Color Test Page

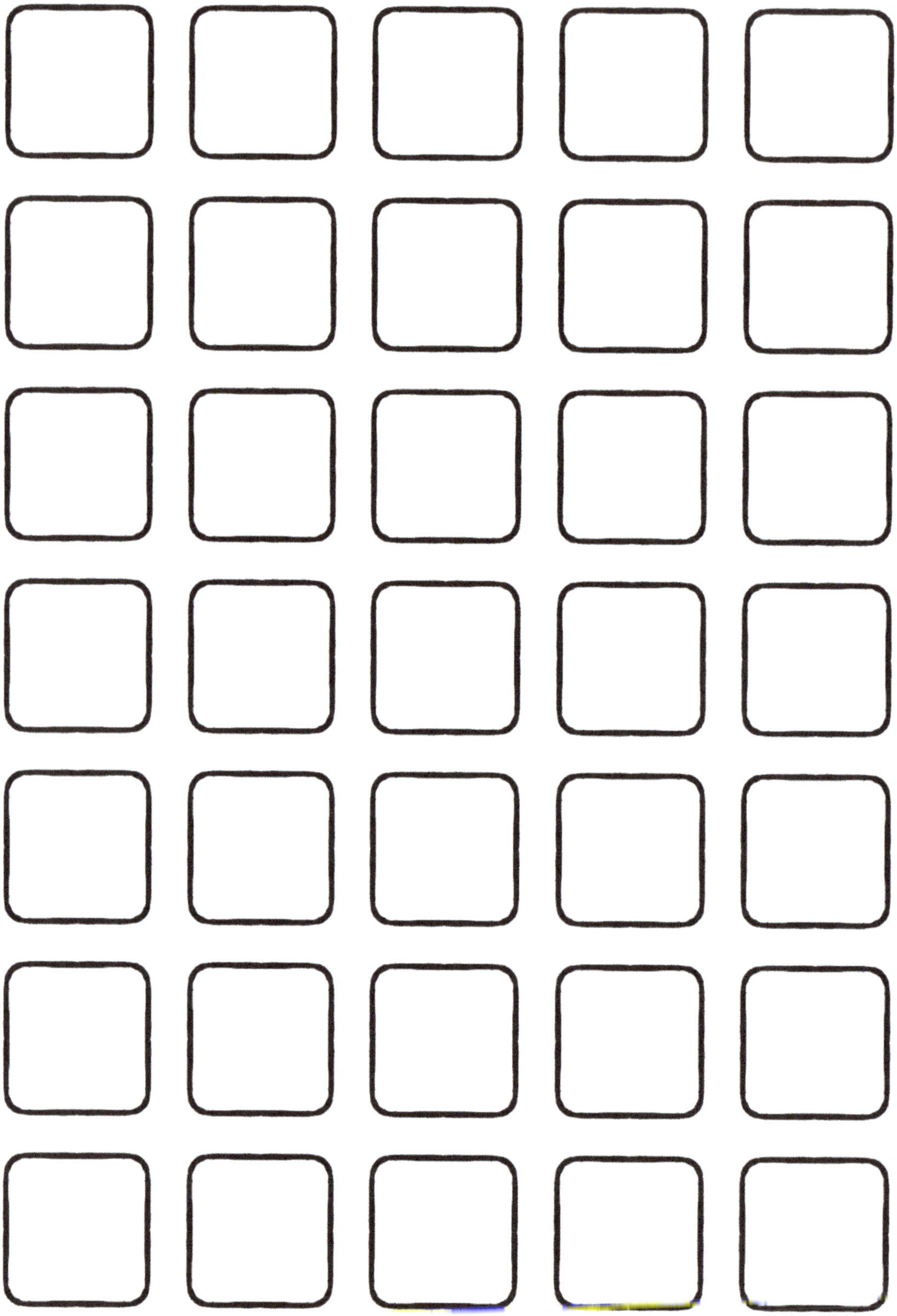

www.ingramcontent.com/pod-product-compliance
Lightning Source LLC
Chambersburg PA
CBHW080507220526
45465CB00006B/2404
* 9 7 9 8 6 6 3 1 6 9 0 0 4 *